CREATOR

SUSTAINER

GOD

PROTECTOR

D1595614

Hajj
THE INNER PILGRIMAGE

by

M. R. Bawa Muhaiyaddeen

THE FELLOWSHIP PRESS
Philadelphia, Pennsylvania

Library of Congress Cataloging-in-Publication Data

Muhaiyaddeen, M. R. Bawa.
    Hajj: the inner pilgrimage / by M. R. Bawa Muhaiyaddeen.
       p. cm.
    Includes index.
    ISBN 0-914390-51-1 (hardcover). — ISBN 0-914390-52-X (trade)
    1. Sufism—Doctrines. 2. Muslim pilgrims and pilgrimages—Saudi
Arabia—Mecca. I. Title.
BP189.3.M86 1998   98-12255
297.3'52—dc21   CIP

Printed in the United States of America
by THE FELLOWSHIP PRESS
Bawa Muhaiyaddeen Fellowship
First Printing

Muhammad Raheem Bawa Muhaiyaddeen ﴿رَضِ﴾

Table of Contents

Foreword

Every ritual act, rather, every action in Islam as in other religions has an inner and an outward aspect. That applies in particular to the great pilgrimage to Mecca which the Muslim is supposed to perform once in his or her life. Its rites look perhaps unusual to a foreign observer, but it is not only the external pilgrimage that human beings are asked to perform, rather, the inner pilgrimage is its important aspect. Nearly a millenium ago a great Persian thinker, Nāsir-i Khusraw, described his reactions to a friend who returned from the pilgrimage without knowing the inner meaning of each and every step that he undertook, and the great poet-philosopher told him that in this case he had not performed the *hajj*.

Thus, in this book, the seeker is taught that the aspects of the *hajj* are manifold and deeply spiritual; the *Ka'bah*, imagined as being just opposite the heavenly *Ka'bah*, can be understood as the human heart which, if properly purified, can be seen as the House of God, and all of our life can be interpreted as the great pilgrimage to the center of life. Not in vain did the major Sufi poets such as Attar use the allegory of the journey—the interior journey—to explain the mysteries of life.

In these days it is necessary—more than before—to emphasize the inner, spiritual aspects of the pilgrimage and the other duties of the believer. I think that Bawa Muhaiyaddeen's new book will be a good help for all those who long to perform the spiritual journey into the heart of hearts where—*in shā' Allāh*—the Divine Beloved can be found.

Annemarie Schimmel

Introduction

Muhammad Raheem Bawa Muhaiyaddeen (may God be pleased with him) was a Sufi *shaikh* from the island country of Sri Lanka, who resided intermittently in the United States from 1971 to his passing in 1986. Bawa Muhaiyaddeen was a mystic who taught the transcendent path of Sufism. He explained that what the world calls real is not reality. We live in an illusory creation. That which we see has a time span and when that time span passes, the physical reality of that which is created dissipates and disappears. Behind the temporary nature of creation there is the permanent nature of God. God does not disappear. God transcends time and space. God is the everlasting truth and the everlasting reality. Yet no man has ever seen God, nor has science been able to give any measure of proof of God. God is known through faith and knowledge of the self. Through all the periods of man's existence, individuals have been sent whose purpose has been to revive faith and to explain who man is and the relationship between man and God. Bawa Muhaiyaddeen was such an individual, a reviver of faith and a teacher and example of the true nature of man.

Much of Bawa Muhaiyaddeen's mystical teachings are explanations of the inner meanings of Islam. This book is a collection of discourses given by Bawa Muhaiyaddeen on the topic of *hajj*. *Hajj* is one of the five obligatory duties of Islam and refers to the pilgrimage to the sacred *Ka'bah* located in the city of Mecca, as divinely ordered in the *Qur'ān*. The five

XII HAJJ: THE INNER PILGRIMAGE

obligatory duties are specifically: 1) the affirmation that there
is no god but God, and Muhammad is the Messenger of God;
2) the five daily prayers; 3) the giving of charity; 4) the fasting during the daylight hours of the month of *Ramadān;* and
5) the pilgrimage to Mecca, known as *hajj.*

To understand the origin and meaning of the various rituals that comprise the *hajj,* it is necessary to first have some
background information as to the origins of the *Ka'bah* and
knowledge of certain events in the lives of the Prophets
Adam ⍨ and Abraham ⍨. When Adam ⍨ and Eve ⍨
were expelled from the Garden of Eden, they were separated
and after wandering for a period of time, were reunited on
the plain of 'Arafāt. The plain of 'Arafāt is located approximately ten miles outside of Mecca. The Angel Gabriel ⍨
was sent to Adam ⍨ and instructed him to build a house in
which to worship God. Adam ⍨, with the guidance of
Gabriel ⍨, constructed this house of God *(Baitullāh)* on the
site where the *Ka'bah* now stands. God sent from heaven a
portion of the heavenly firmament which when it came to
earth was a white stone. This white stone was set in one of
the corners of the house of worship. This stone became
blackened by the sins of the mortal beings who touched it
and is now known as the Black Stone. The ritual of
circumambulation of the *Ka'bah,* known as *tawāf,* was
taught to Adam ⍨ by Gabriel ⍨. Symbolically, *tawāf* is
explained as an earthly re-creation of the heavenly practice
of the angels worshiping God by circumambulating His
throne. It is tied to the nature of all things, from the earth
orbiting the sun, to the moon orbiting the earth, to the spin-
ning of electrons around the nucleus of an atom.

When Abraham ⍨ was asked by his wife, Sarah ⍨, to
remove his handmaiden Hagar ⍨ from their household

along with Abraham and Hagar's son, Ishmael (☞),
Abraham (☞) traveled to the exact spot where the *Ka'bah* had
originally been built but had been destroyed by the great
flood of Noah (☞). There, Abraham (☞) left Hagar (☞) and
their small child, Ishmael (☞). Hagar (☞) soon ran out of water, and ran between two small hills known as Safā and
Marwah looking for water. As she ran between the two hills,
water sprung from the ground where she had placed the infant Ishmael (☞). This well, which still gushes forth water in
abundance, was named *zamzam* by Hagar (☞).

As Ishmael (☞) grew, Abraham (☞) visited him often. On
one of these visits, Abraham (☞) was instructed by God to
sacrifice Ishmael (☞). As Abraham (☞) made arrangements
for the sacrifice, satan came to him and told Abraham (☞)
that his messages were not divine revelations, but rather hal-
lucinations of his own mind. Abraham (☞) rejected satan.
Prior to the sacrifice taking place, God intervened and a ram
was brought by angels to be sacrificed instead of Ishmael (☞).
God indicated to Abraham (☞) that this had been a test of his
faith. Later, Abraham (☞) was directed to rebuild the *Ka'bah,*
and he was further directed that this was to become a place
of pilgrimage for all mankind. Abraham (☞) and Ishmael (☞)
rebuilt the *Ka'bah* in the location where it had originally
been built by Adam (☞). The location of the *zamzam* well is
less than fifty feet from the *Ka'bah,* and the small hills, Safā
and Marwah, are within five hundred feet of the *Ka'bah.*
Today, the *Ka'bah,* the well, and the hills are all within the
confines of the Grand Mosque of Mecca. The locations
where Abraham (☞) rejected the three temptations by satan
are in an area known as Minā. All of these locations and
events are integral to the rituals involved in the *hajj.*

The Prophet Muhammad (☞), during his tenth year in the

city of Medina, gathered his followers and made pilgrimage to Mecca and the *Ka'bah,* following the instruction previously given to Abraham ☺ by God. The *hajj* is a re-creation of the pilgrimage made by Muhammad ☺ and the acts performed during *hajj* are in accordance with the customs as established by Muhammad ☺.

One prepares for *hajj* as if one were preparing for death. Prior to leaving for *hajj,* it is customary to conclude all of one's worldly affairs, pay off all one's debts, and write one's will. The *hajj* is begun by consecrating oneself and entering a pure state known as *ihrām.* While in this state, many mundane permitted acts of daily life become forbidden. The pilgrim dons a costume also known as the *ihrām.* The *ihrām* is symbolic of a funeral shroud. For men, the *ihrām* consists of two unstitched and seamless pieces of cloth. Each piece of cloth (usually toweling) is about three feet wide by up to seven feet long. One piece is draped around the waist, in sarong-like fashion, and the other is draped over the left shoulder and knotted near the waist. The right shoulder remains exposed. Women usually wear a white dress-like garment which covers their body from the neck to the wrists to the ankles. Women also wear a head covering which covers their hair entirely and allows only the face to show.

The major rituals of *hajj* begin with *tawāf,* which consists of circumambulating the *Ka'bah* seven times in prayerful meditation. The pilgrim *(hajji)* then offers two cycles of ritual prayer *(rak'ah)* and proceeds to the *zamzam* well to drink of its water. Thereafter, the ceremony of *Sa'y* is performed. *Sa'y* consists of traveling back and forth seven times between the hills of Safā and Marwah, as Hagar ☺ did in her search for water for her infant child, Ishmael ☺. After the completion of *Sa'y,* the pilgrim travels to and spends the night at Mīnā, an area about five miles outside of Mecca. The next day the pilgrim moves to the plain of 'Arafāt where the day is spent in prayer and contemplation. In the evening, the pilgrim moves on to Muzdalifa, an area adjacent to the plain of 'Arafāt where the evening is spent in worship. The next morning, the pilgrim goes from Muzdalifa back to Mīnā where the ceremony of throwing pebbles at satan is performed. The throwing of the pebbles signifies Abraham's rejections of satan's attempted interference with God's instructions to sacrifice Ishmael ☙. The pilgrim then returns to the Grand Mosque in Mecca and performs *tawāf* again, and then returns to Mīnā to repeat the ceremony of stoning the devil. Finally, the pilgrim returns to the *Ka'bah* to perform the farewell *tawāf,* signifying completion of the *hajj.* A detailed description of all the rituals comprising *hajj* and the manner in which they are to be performed is set forth in the *sharī'at,* the Islamic canon law.

In Bawa Muhaiyaddeen's teachings he explains the *sharī'at* as our outer life. First, we must understand what is permissible and what is not permissible in the outer life. All that is of the world is ruled by *sharī'at.* After we learn to embrace that which is correct and reject that which is forbidden and develop strong faith, certitude, and determination in God, we can proceed on the transcendent path. This next phase is called *tarīqat.* In this state we have contentment in every circumstance with whatever is provided, and in every instance we give all praise to God, saying, *"Al-hamdu lillāh!"* The third state is known as *haqīqat. Haqīqat* is to begin to know that Beautiful One. There is only One God to whom worship belongs, and in *haqīqat* realization of the Divine occurs as well as the beginnings of communication with God. The next step is *ma'rifat. Ma'rifat* is the light that contains no day and no night. Merging with that light is *ma'rifat*. The final step is called *sūfiyyat,* the place where one disappears into God, Allah, in the same way that firewood no longer exists after being burned and only the fire remains.

We live in a state of form, our bodies. Yet within our bodies there is our true self which is mysteriously interconnected, yet separate from our bodies. The world is illusory, but it is within this illusory realm that our body exists, and while we are in the time span of our body, we are subject to the physical laws of the *sharī'at.* The outer performance of the obligatory actions in Islam, including the performance of *hajj,* are the obligations of our physical form. The inner path is the understanding of that which is beyond the physical body and the path of transformation from a physical being to a light being. To die to this world before the physical death takes place is the Sufi way of life. The discourses that make up this book are explanations of the inner transformation that must take place within man in order for man to follow the path toward God. The outer obligations are examples for the inner transformation. Through participating in the outer obligations, the inner transformation is aided.

The ritual of *tawāf* is unique to the *Ka'bah.* It is not only one of the main rituals of *hajj,* but goes on constantly, day and night, around the *Ka'bah,* except during formal prayer. The following is an attempt to convey some of the sights, sounds, and experiences that occur during the performance of *tawāf.*

TAWĀF

Holy Shrine
Outside of time
Dressed in black

Mortal beings
Heartfelt pleadings
Dressed in white

Gold gilded door
White marble floor
Heaven's own white/black stone

White shrouds abound
Circling round
Chanting prayers

Heavenly dance
Prayers enhanced
Rising up

Focused glance
Prayerful trance
Singing praise

Cries out loud
From the shrouds
Seeking grace

Beloved Lord
You've seen and heard
All that we hide

Accept our plea
Set the guilty free
Saved from the fire

Attachments lost
Illusion crossed
Subhānallāh[1]

All praise to Him
Without kin
Alone and One

Yā Rahmān Yā Rahīm
Yā Rahmān Yā Rahīm
Ihdinās-sirātal-mustaqīm[2]

Prior to the performance of the various rituals during *hajj,*
it is customary to set an intention that focuses on the act that
is about to take place and the purpose for the performance
of the act. In accordance with that tradition, the following
words are set forth to help set an intention for the reading
of this book.

RECITE

Recite, what has been told
Recite in awe, the grandeur bold

---

1. All glory be to God.
2. O Most Merciful One, O Most Compassionate One
   O Most Merciful One, O Most Compassionate One
   Show us the straight path.

Recite the words of praise
Recite to lift the haze
Recite the words that quell desire
Recite the words that put out fire
Recite silently, without sound
Recite so angels around you abound
Recite the vibrations of the names of the Lord
Recite the resonance of the eternal chord
Recite to surrender the need to resist
Recite to surrender the will to exist
Recite to become the words you recite
Recite to become one with the Light

And now with intention set, proceed on the inner pilgrimage with Bawa Muhaiyaddeen as your guide. May his words
resonate within your hearts and clear the path for transformation and transcendence.

Mūsa Muhaiyaddeen
(Emanuel L. Levin, Esq.)

Editor's Note

The discourses selected for this collection on the inner meaning of *hajj* were given by Muhammad Raheem Bawa Muhaiyaddeen ⟨圆⟩ in Colombo, Sri Lanka and in Philadelphia, Pennsylvania, U.S.A., between 1978-1985. Many were given on *'Īdul-Adhā,* the three days of celebration marking the end of the pilgrimage.

Originally spoken in Tamil, interspersed with Arabic terminology, these talks were translated by Mrs. Rajes Ganesan, Mrs. Crisi Beutler, Dr. Usha Balamore, Dr. K. Ganesan, Dr. M. Z. Markar, and Mr. T. K. B. Rahman, and then edited by Mrs. Rajes Ganesan, Dr. Howard Posner, and Mrs. Karin Marcus. The cover and artwork were done by Mr. Lawrence Didona, as inspired by the text. All who worked on this project humbly ask forgiveness for any clarity or vitality lost in the process.

Bawa Muhaiyaddeen's use of Arabic terminology was both intentional and purposeful. Although these words are common throughout the Islamic world, Bawa Muhaiyaddeen's usage frequently encompasses deeper mystical meanings. All these terms have been italicized in the text and a glossary at the back of the book provides extensive definitions. To help the Western reader, simplified translations of these terms have periodically been included in the text. Also to enhance readability, the customary honorific phrases spoken after the names of prophets, angels, and saints are denoted by calligraphic circles. Their meanings can also be found in the glossary.

The depth and breadth of Bawa Muhaiyaddeen's teachings cannot be contained within any man-made vessel. In producing this book, the volunteers of the Fellowship Press offer their best effort in the hope that those who read it will be inspired to search deeper and deeper.

1
The Final Hajj of Prophet Muhammad ﷺ

My love you, my children, my daughters, my sons, my grandchildren, my brothers and sisters. According to the Arabic calendar, last night the pilgrims completed their *hajj* in Mecca, and today is the time for celebration.

Near the end of his life, the *Rasūl* (the Messenger, Prophet Muhammad ﷺ) traveled from Medina to Mecca and fulfilled his final *hajj*. The *Rasūl* ﷺ and his followers had been chased out of Mecca. Their lands and homes had been seized, and for many years, numerous injustices had been committed against them by the people of Mecca. They were beaten and driven away. Some were even murdered.

At that time, there were three hundred and sixty idols and forty-eight thousand statues housed in the *Ka'bah*[1] and in the surrounding area. There were three hundred and thirty million statues of gods *(dēvas)*, forty-eight thousand idols of ascetics *(rishis)*, and three hundred and sixty large idols. The people denied the existence of God and worshiped dogs, foxes, and the energies of the earth, air, fire, water, and ether. They worshiped the energies of animals, birds, dogs, foxes, horses, donkeys, snakes, scorpions, eagles, and vultures. They made all the creatures opposite to God into gods and worshiped them. They did not know the difference between

---

1. In the religion of Islam, the *Ka'bah* is both the most important shrine of worship and the symbol of the unity of worship of all believers. One of the five *furūd* (obligatory duties) of Islam is the pilgrimage *(hajj)* to the *Ka'bah*. It is a cube-like building in the center of the mosque in Mecca.

good and evil. They worshiped arrogance, *karma,* and *māyā.*[2] They turned these objects of worship, these false gods, into their protectors, creators, and nourishers, claiming that these idols protected and sustained them and watched over their births and deaths. They believed that these idols would grant them heaven. Like this, they kept and worshiped so many separate things.

In those days, there were many murders and killings; the people sacrificed animals such as cows, goats, and chickens, and even human beings. They performed blood sacrifices and many kinds of rituals *(pūjās).* They would offer these sacrifices and pour the blood over the idols. It was a time of ignorance, a time without mercy. Female children were commonly buried alive, while male children were taught the skills and arts of combat, so that they could become warriors and commit still more thefts, atrocities, and murders. They were trained as warriors on the evil path.

During the time of Abraham ☞ this place was cleared and a mosque was built. It was here that the Angel Gabriel ☞ brought forth the *zamzam* water and gave it to Ishmael ☞ and Hagar ☞. Hagar ☞ was alone in the desert, frantically searching for water. Her child was crying, and there was no water anywhere. Then God told Gabriel ☞ to descend. He came on a white horse, and when the horse's hoof struck the ground, the water flowed.

---

2. *karma*—The inherited qualities formed at the time of conception; the qualities of the essences of the five elements; the qualities of the mind; the qualities of the connection to hell.

māyā—Illusion; the unreality of the visible world; the glitters seen in the darkness of illusion; the 105 million glitters seen in the darkness of the mind which result in 105 million rebirths. *Māyā* is an elemental energy, or *shakti,* which takes on various shapes, causes man to forfeit his wisdom, and confuses and hypnotizes him into a state of torpor.

Allah[3] told Gabriel ﷺ to give this water to Ishmael ﷺ as a blessing *(barakat)*, and that well is still there today.

When Hagar ﷺ came running back from her search, she saw someone in the distance and cried out, "Who is taking my child!"

Gabriel ﷺ was standing over the child saying, "O Ishmael, Allah said that this is the *zamzam* well. Its fragrant water can wash away the dirt and dispel the darkness of the heart. It is the water of Allah's grace *(rahmat)* which was created by His power *(qudrat)*. It was created for you by Allah. It was created for the straight path. This water will continuously flow in abundance and will never dry up." Gabriel ﷺ told him this, and then disappeared, leaving Ishmael ﷺ gazing happily up at the sky. When Hagar ﷺ reached him, she saw the child smiling at the sky and the water flowing. The mosque of the *Ka'bah* was built around this spot.

The *Ka'bah* was built as a central place for the four directions. It was the center for the four sections of earth, air, fire, and water. Just as man was created out of earth, air, fire, water, and ether with the heart *(qalb)* in the center of the body, the *Ka'bah* was built in the center of the four directions of the world. God instructed Abraham ﷺ to begin the construction of this building and to finish it as well. It was destroyed after Abraham's time, but other prophets came to rebuild it according to Allah's word. Later, Muhammad ﷺ came, replaced the stone, and rebuilt the *Ka'bah* once more. This same place is called the *Ka'bah* today. Even though it is built out of stone, it is the central point. It exists as a focal point that guides people on the straight path and inspires them to have faith and trust in God.

---

3. Allah or *Allāhu* is the Arabic word for God, the One and Only; the One of infinite grace and incomparable love; the Eternal, Effulgent One.

During the time of Abraham ☪, the idols had been thrown out of the *Ka'bah,* but later, they were gathered and reinstated as gods. People thought these elemental energies *(shaktis)* and idols of ignorance could protect them, but they had even less potentialities than human beings *(insān).* People made gods out of these energies that were greatly inferior to man's wisdom and faith and to the grace of his divine qualities and beseeched these gods to protect them.

In that very same land, Allah created that Prophet ☪ again,[4] as the son of 'Abdullāh, as a Messenger of God, a Prophet, a *Rasūl* to the world, a light to the heart, and a strength to *īmān* (unshakable faith). God created him as the Prophet ☪ with great strength and certitude and as one who could help people establish a connection to Allah. He came to dispel the darkness of the heart, destroy ignorance, dispel arrogance and *karma,* destroy separations and differences, and bring about unity and peace. It was through these qualities that God enabled Muhammad ☪ to attract people. The mosque was also built for this purpose.

The *Ka'bah* is the central point of the four directions in the world, just as the heart *(qalb)* is the central point within the body. There are eighteen thousand universes in man, are there not? The heart is the central place for all that. The heart is the source of prayer, and the *Ka'bah,* the mosque, is also a source of prayer. To one who understands, the heart will be the *Ka'bah.* For those who do not understand, this *Ka'bah* was built as proof, so that they could realize this section.

When the *Rasūl* ☪ revealed this truth, he and his follow-

---

4. In Chapter One of *A Song of Muhammad* ☪, Bawa Muhaiyaddeen explains that Muhammad ☪ appeared as an enlightened being in each of the four religions, his final appearance being in the religion of Islam.

ers were chased, beaten, tortured, and murdered. Their freedom and property were seized. They were exiled and then
pursued wherever they went. People repeatedly tried to
murder them. During all this, they kept the *Ka'bah* within
their hearts and Allah within that *Ka'bah*. They kept the
truth within Allah and prayer within that truth. From that
prayer, they received the strength of *īmān* and certitude.
From within this and through Him, they acquired His
qualities and wisdom. Having acquired these, they left the
land of Mecca carrying the *Ka'bah,* the truth, within.

They underwent so many injustices and hardships. There
were so many murders and killings, horrible things that they
could not bear. There were people who would travel back
and forth carrying tales just to increase the enmity between
the two groups. Some people would come to Medina and
spread rumors, hoping to start fights. Then they would return to Mecca and spread more rumors and cause still more
fighting and destruction.

Some who followed the *Rasūl* 🕌 were very clever, courageous, and strong. They had always been greatly respected
in Mecca. After they were exiled and had settled in Medina,
these tales disturbed them. They felt dishonored, disgraced,
and ashamed. "We left our city, our possessions, and our
land, and now they are treating us with such indignity. They
are killing our wives and children and destroying everything. How can we live in this state?"

The Prophet's followers came and cried to the *Rasūlullāh* 🕌,
"*Yā Rasūlullāh,* you are the Messenger of Allah, you are a
Prophet. You do not contain the world. You do not have any
thought of fighting, of quarreling, or of separation. All your
possessions and your freedom belong to Allah. But, we have
not yet attained that state. We must protect our dignity and

honor, so that we are not disgraced. It is shameful for us to always run away when we are repeatedly attacked by the Meccans. We feel ashamed. We are unable to face this. We are human beings. We are not like you. God has not yet brought us to your state. We are left with a feeling of humiliation instead of honor. We must oppose those who are attacking us. You must give us permission to fight and wage war against them. We must be allowed to retaliate against those who are attacking us. The more we run and hide, the more they keep chasing us and killing us. How can we live with this shame? How can we bear this disgrace? Our women and children are being beaten, raped, and killed. This is so unjust. How can our hearts bear this? *Yā Rasūlullāh,* God gave that state to you, but we have still not given up the world. We must protect our honor. Give us permission to do this. We must live with dignity or die with dignity."

Some of Muhammad's companions and followers spoke like this, but the *Rasūl* ﷺ did not reply at that time. He was silent. Many months went by. Repeatedly, they came to him with this plea. Years went by and still they begged him, saying, "We cannot bear this."

Then the *Rasūl* ﷺ explained, "This is Allah's command. I do not like fighting or war. It is our duty to protect the sanctity that Allah is One and to protect man *(insān).* It is man's duty to protect his *īmān,* wisdom, and Allah's qualities. This is the correct way. Within ourselves, we should protect our faith in Allah and our intention for Him. We must protect His exalted qualities within us. We must protect His wisdom, His tranquility, and His justice within us. We must protect God's actions—they must not be destroyed! The purpose of the *īmān* known as Islam is to protect us from being destroyed by satans, demons, devils, ghosts, evil qualities, blood-sucking beings, deceit, treachery, envy, resentment, jealousy, anger, arrogance, and all such evils. This is the purpose of unity and the qualities of God. You are my brothers. This is the only treasure you must protect, nothing else. This is the sole treasure. It is by protecting the qualities of God that you protect your dignity. You must protect your goodness. You must protect the treasury of God, His grace. That is how to protect your honor. If you protect your tongue and eyes from evil, that will be the repository of God's grace. If you protect your ears, nose, and heart, and God's treasures, you will have protected the benefits of the divine kingdom of God's love, His kingdom (*ākhirah*).

"Truth is His kingdom, goodness is His scepter, justice is His throne, and patience is the state from which His kingdom is ruled. Compassion is His state. This is the earth upon which God walks. If you do not protect this, you will lose this state. You should not think of this world as the source of your honor. All the base desires (*nafs ammārah*) and demons are within us. Some people raise them externally, while others raise them internally. Some nourish evil outside, and some nourish it inside. What does it matter? When one nourishes evil on the inside, he kills with his thoughts, day by day. The other kills externally, week by week. Both are murderers.

"Who is good? A man of goodness is one who protects the treasures of Allah. He is one who has honor. He is one who has the wealth of God's grace (*daulat*). A wealthy man is one who protects the grace (*rahmat*) and qualities of Allah. One who protects these is in *Īmān-Islām*.[5] He is the one who follows

---

5. *Īmān-Islām*—The state of the spotlessly pure heart which contains Allah's Holy *Qur'ān*. His divine radiance, His divine wisdom, His truth, His prophets, His angels, and His laws. The pure heart which, having cut away all evil, takes on the power of that courageous determination called *īmān* and stands shining in the resplendence of Allah.

God and the messengers. Allah has spoken these words. Do not be sad about what is happening. Allah is the One who must protect us. We must protect His treasures, and He must protect what He has to protect. If we let these treasures drop from our hands, then Allah will also let go of the treasure that He protects."

The *Rasūl* ﷺ spoke to his followers about the firm strength and valor of *īmān* and truth. They heard this, but they were still young. The aspects of the world, the earth, air, fire, water, ether, mind, and desire were still operating within them. So much backbiting and gossiping was going back and forth, concerning what was happening in both cities. Because their blood was boiling, the Prophet's followers repeatedly asked for permission to fight. They told the *Rasūl* ﷺ of how their wives were raped, their children were slaughtered, and their brothers and sisters were abused.

Still the *Rasūl* ﷺ replied, "My heart does not feel that way. Only when Allah grants His permission can you proceed. Allah sent me to destroy that which destroys the state of the true self. What destroys the self? It is not your brothers and sisters. What is it that destroys the self, the truth of the life, what you gathered from the divine kingdom (*ākhirah*) and from this world? You should destroy the things that are destroying your search for compassion, truth, wisdom, and worship (*'ibādat*), the search for the love for Allah, His justice, and His qualities. Anyone who tries to take away this treasure that is our exalted search for Him, anyone who tries to dispel unity, love, tolerance, patience, and peace—anyone who tries to destroy this state must be destroyed. You can fight anyone who comes to plunder these treasures. To destroy him, use the sword of faith, sharpened with wisdom, and the courage of your love for Allah. You

*T*he Ka'bah is the central point of the four directions in the world, just as the heart (qalb) is the central point within the body. There are eighteen thousand universes in man, are there not? The heart is the central place for all that. The heart is the source of prayer, and the Ka'bah, the mosque, is also a source of prayer. To one who understands, the heart will be the Ka'bah. For those who do not understand, this Ka'bah was built as proof, so that they could realize this section.

—M. R. BAWA MUHAIYADDEEN

can fight him in that way, but you cannot fight anyone else. When it is said that you can fight anyone who comes to take your treasure, the treasure being referred to is your love for Allah and the beauty of His qualities. In one's life they are like a beautiful maiden, a child of love with the beauty of wisdom, the wealth of compassion, and the blissful state of patience. Allah has said that anyone who comes to destroy these things should be destroyed. He did not tell us to destroy our brothers and sisters.

"These inner treasures are your true wealth. You can destroy those who come to seize your inner treasures, but not those who come to seize the wealth of earth, air, fire, water, ether, mind, and desire. Those are the very things which destroy you! Allah never said to fight for those things. You should fight those things that come to destroy the goodness within. They are your enemies. Fight them! The plundering of your land and gold, your blood ties and ancestral heritage, or other material things has nothing to do with your dignity. It is the treasures of God that are your honor and dignity. It is these inner treasures that you must protect with respect and love. To lose those treasures is a loss of dignity, a disgrace! You should reflect. This is what Allah has said.

"Allah never told you to wound or kill your brothers and sisters. If you behave as they behave, then what is the difference between you? If they kill your child, brothers, or sisters and take your possessions, it is not correct for you to do the same thing in return. Is this honor and dignity? Allah never told anyone to act like that. Think about this." This is what the *Rasūl* ⟨ﷺ⟩ told his followers. But again, some deceitful and treacherous people carried tales back and forth. And upon hearing these, the hearts of his followers were once again turbulent with sorrow and distress. Again, they thought only of their wives, their children, their livestock, and their possessions. Some still regarded this state a disgrace. Again, they were told, "You must understand what is truly yours in this world. Only if they take that treasure must you fight."

Finally, the permission to fight came from Allah. One hundred and fourteen conditions were laid down concerning how they should conduct themselves in battle. "You should only fight with someone who wields a sword against you. If his sword breaks, you should not continue to fight with him. If the person you are fighting falls, you should not strike him. But if someone tries to strangle you, you can strangle him back. If he takes your property, you can challenge him. Even then, you should not touch his wife, children, trees, livestock, or farm. They are not causing you any harm." Like this, one hundred and fourteen rules were given before they were allowed to fight. Anyone who deviated from any of these rules would be considered a murderer and would be subject to Allah's questioning.

Protecting the inner treasure is the only battle waged for God. This means killing the evils which come to kill you on the inside. But if you fight for outer things, you will be doing the work of hell and committing murder. Allah will question you about this. If you wage the war within, the war against satan, the war against the animals within, the war against the ghosts and desires *(nafs ammārah)*, then that is the true holy war. If the world within you is made to die, you will receive eternal life *(hayāt)* in the divine world *(ākhirah)*. But if you torment and torture others for the sake of worldly goods, then you must face questioning on the Day of Judgment and face the sufferings of hell. Those things are not His wealth; they were discarded by Him. You have to understand this and obtain His treasure.

The *Rasūlullāh* 🕊 said, "Allah has ordained these rules." And they went to battle in accordance with the words of Allah. But the *Rasūlullāh* 🕊 did not hurt anyone. To him the word *Bismillāhir-Rahmānir-Rahīm* (In the name of God, the Most Merciful, Most Compassionate) was given by Allah as the magnanimous sword of faith, the sword of justice. It was not a knife or sword forged from iron. It was forged from Allah's love, from the grace and justice of Allah. Muhammad 🕊 was the only one who could wield this sword. Others could not even see it. It was not a blade made of steel. It was made with Allah's truth, wisdom, strength, and faith.

The Meccans came to fight on camels and on horses. They came to battle drunk, carrying all their provisions and deities. The followers of the *Rasūl* 🕊 were imploring, "O God!" and reciting a verse from the *Qur'ān*. "*Alif, lām, mīm. Allāhu lā ilāha illā huwal-hayyul-qayyūm.*"[6] Everyone was reciting this *sūrat*. Everyone was pleading, "O God, forgive us, save us from this." They were making this supplication (*du'ā'*). "Change them, bring them to the straight path. O God, accept us. Allah, stop this fighting. Bring them to the good path." This was the state that the *Rasūl* 🕊 had spoken about.

Once all the fighting stopped, the Meccans realized the truth. With Allah's *salām* (greetings of peace) and with His *salawāt* (blessings) resonating, the fighting halted. Allah's love, the *salām,* and the *salawāt* resonated throughout the land. The serene state of inner patience (*sabūr*) was outspread, *īmān* became strong, wisdom evolved, faith, certi-

---

6. *Sūrat Āl 'Imrān, Sūrat III,* verses 1 and 2. *Alif, lām, mīm* are three mystical letters which open the *sūrat; Allāhu lā ilāha illā huwal-hayyul-qayyūm:* God! There is no god but He—the Living, the Self-subsisting, Eternal.

tude, determination, and peace flourished and the people rejoiced. With this resonance, they finally approached the *Ka'bah.* When the battles were fought with swords and knives, the Meccans won. But when the followers approached in this exalted state, the Meccans could not defeat them. When they came carrying their love for Allah, faith, wisdom, and Allah's *salām* and *salawāt,* when they were armed with Allah's weapons, the Meccans could not defeat them. When they carried patience *(sabūr)* with them, they could not be defeated. The Meccans listened to the *salām* and *salawāt,* they witnessed the patience and the trust in God *(tawakkul),* the love and compassion, and they could not defeat them. They could not conquer those who had faith. They realized that their gods, their idols, their qualities, swords, horses, and armies could not win. They surrendered and accepted Allah and *īmān.* It is with these weapons that the Prophet ﷺ and his followers approached the *Ka'bah* and finally performed the *hajj.*

What is *hajj?* It is to destroy separation and dispel ignorance, to bring about peace, tranquility, serenity, unity, love, harmony, and to know that God is love. Without deviating from virtue, truth, and the state of bliss, to know with certainty that God is One and that there is one family, to become one with *Allāhu* and to establish that state is *hajj.* It is to proceed in unity as one family, one people, with One God and one prayer, to dedicate oneself to Him, to surrender to Him, to make the world within die, giving life *(hayāt)* to His grace, His wealth, and His treasures. He decreed that *hajj* is to give life to *īmān* and these treasures, to make that *hayāt* one's own. This is the state of *hajj,* the state of glorifying Allah. Toward the end, in his final days, before he left the world and changed, the *Rasūl* ﷺ performed the *hajj* of dying before death.

Hajj is to die before death. This is the meaning of *hajj*—
the world within you dies and the good qualities come alive;
you bring them to Allah and merge with Him. *Hajj* is to go
forth with unity, love, harmony, and peace, with the thought
of one family, one people, one prayer, and One God, and to
merge with Allah. *Hajj* is the fifth *fard* (oligatory duty)[7] of
Īmān-Islām. This is what is called *hajj*. In that state, the
Rasūl 🕊️ spoke these words. "You can belong to any religion,
any caste, or any race. You can be of any group. There is
nothing to those things. They do not matter. Your state must
be unity and love. However you pray, you must live with the
treasures of unity, harmony, compassion, love, patience, and
peace. Allah said to do this. I am a human being and you are
human beings. Only Allah knows what will happen to me
tomorrow. I am willing to participate in what you are doing.
When you do good, I am ready to take part in that. But when
you do evil, I will move away. I will not join in that, but I
will share in your unity and harmony and in your good
qualities. It is God's qualities that bring us together in unity.
I do not share in satan's qualities of the 'I' and the 'you', mine
and yours, my possessions and your possessions, my house
and your house, my caste and your caste, my language and
your language. I will join with you and take part in Allah's
speech, His unity, compassion, patience, love, His peace, and
in all His qualities. I will take part in these. All of us must
join together and share in these things. Our hearts must take
part in these qualities.

"This is the exalted state for us. Each one must understand

---

7. *fard* (pl. *furūd*)—The five obligatory duties *(furūd)* known as the five
pillars of Islam: *ash-shahādah* (witnessing that there is no god but God, and
Muhammad is the Messenger of God), prayer, charity, fasting, and holy
pilgrimage *(hajj)*.

and act accordingly. Your sorrows are my sorrows and my sorrows are yours. Your hunger is mine and my hunger is yours. Your pain is my pain and my pain is yours. Your happiness is mine and my happiness is yours. Your praise is my praise and my praise is yours. Anything that happens to you happens to me. You must firmly establish this state in unity. Allah accepts those who live with this unity, no matter what group they belong to. This is love, this is unity, this is prayer, this is worship, and these are the qualities which accept and love Allah. Each one of you must act accordingly. The end of my time in the world is near. I have fulfilled the words and actions commanded by Allah. After me, you are the ones who must fulfill this. You have to foster that unity.

"The *Ka'bah* is the central place. Through Abraham (☞) and the prophets that came before and after him, God has revealed this as the source or the cause and the heart as the effect. The house of the heart is the place of worship. This is the *Ka'bah,* a very important place for prayer. The *Ka'bah* symbolizes unity and love. In this place, we must receive the love of God. This is *hajj,* the fifth *fard* (obligatory duty). Think of this.

"Unity is *hajj,* love is *hajj,* the qualities and actions of God are *hajj.* His wisdom is *hajj.* Establishing patience (*sabūr*), contentment (*shakūr*), trust in God (*tawakkul*), and unshakable faith (*īmān*) is *hajj.* To bring about peace and wisdom is *hajj.* To see the divine world (*ākhirah*) within yourself and to realize all of the qualities of Allah is *hajj.* Unity and love are *hajj.*

"Allah will answer any heart that is filled with this love and unity. Anyone whose heart attains such a state is accepted by Allah. The resonance comes from His grace and resplendence, saying, 'I accept you.' This world then becomes the divine world. The wealth of the divine world is given to them in completeness while in this world. When that state comes, this is *hajj*. You and I must reflect upon this."

These are some of the last words that the *Rasūl* ﷺ spoke before he left this world. This is related in many ways in the traditional accounts *(ahādīth)* and in his discourses. When he fulfilled the *hajj,* he revealed many explanations.

Today is the celebration of the *hajj*. It is the day that the fifth *fard* (obligatory duty) was fulfilled by the *Rasūl* ﷺ. Today is the *hajj* festival, when all our suffering and sorrows are dispelled. We live in unity, with happiness, peacefulness, love, compassion, and trust. We have that love for one another. We join in unity and love. Today is the day that we join together in happiness. We forget all the separations, disputes, and sorrows that we have experienced, and we celebrate our happiness.

After the *Rasūl* ﷺ spoke these words, those who had been in ignorance affirmed their *īmān* and embraced peace, unity, love, and compassion. Mecca became one in Islam. This was the time of acceptance, the time of *hajj,* a very blissful time. This is what was called *hajj*. This was the *hajj* festival. When all united and prayed to Allah, that was *hajj,* that was prayer *(toluhai)* and devotion *('ibādat)*. When everyone joined together in that good state with love, embracing each other, heart to heart, dispelling their sorrows, their problems, and their separations, when all came together and embraced each other, heart to heart, looked at each other face to face, embraced with love, and gave *salāms*—that was *hajj*. It was the day when sorrows, differences, and sufferings ended, and all the wounds and hurts were healed. Evil, enmity, and treachery were chased away. It was the day of joy.

On this day of the fifth *fard* (obligatory duty) of *hajj*, all the
sorrow we have experienced, all the sorrow, the ignorance,
the suffering, and the separations of the world, the 'I' and the
'you' are destroyed. This is the day of the fifth *fard*, the day
of peace when all join together. This is the day of the *hajj* festival. This happiness is this festival. This unity and love are
the festival. If we open our hearts with love toward Him and
praise Him, that is the day of prayer. This is the *hajj* festival.

My love you, my grandchildren. Each one of you must
think about this state. No matter what race, religion, or caste
you are, you must have this peace, this unity, compassion,
love, tranquility, and all the qualities of God. You must embrace each other in this state, heart to heart, and gaze at each
other's face, speaking His names and His words and acting
according to His actions, His ninety-nine attributes *(wilāyāt)*,
His compassion and love. You must acquire the ability to
embrace these qualities, accept the truth, and act accordingly
with love. Then no matter what religion you are, it is acceptable to Allah. But you must try to understand the difference
between good and evil and extract only the good. You must
join together and do this, no matter to what group you belong. Acquire this state of peace, tranquility, unity, justice,
compassion, patience, and tolerance. Acquire the loving
qualities of God, live in unity, have love for Allah, join your
hearts to Him, and unite with Him. If you exist in this state,
He will make this world into the divine kingdom *(ākhirah)*.
You will dwell in the freedom and happiness of heaven. This
is certain. This is the absolute truth. These are the words
given to the prophets. You must think about this. You must
have this certitude of *īmān*. With wisdom and love, you must
praise God and show compassion to everyone. Then the

world will be made into heaven for you. In your life, you will have peace, tranquility, light, and beauty. God will protect you. *Āmīn, āmīn.*

Understand this. *Āmīn.* Allah is sufficient unto us all.

As-salāmu 'alaikum wa rahmatullāhi wa barakātuhu. Anbu. May the peace and blessings of Allah be upon you. I give you my love.

September 28, 1982

2
The True Fulfillment of Hajj

*B*ismillāhir-Rahmānir-Rahīm. (In the name of God, the Most Merciful, Most Compassionate.) This is the 1,402nd year of the *hajj,* the pilgrimage which comes two months after *Ramadān* (the holy month of fasting). All of you have finished the *hajj* prayers and come. In Islam this is an important duty, the fifth and final *fard* (obligatory duty).

In the history of Islam, the *hajj* is given great importance. Within the *kalimah*[1] and in the *Rasūl's* ﷺ teachings, this is the most important duty. Of the five *furūd* (obligatory duties), the first four are easy for a human being *(insān)* to fulfill, but, if we understand *hajj* in the proper way, this fifth duty is very difficult. It concerns both life and death. If we reflect with wisdom upon what is required to fulfill this *fard* and analyze this with *īmān* and with Allah's qualities, then we will realize how extremely difficult it is.

All of everything experiences life and death. In life and in death, the way to fulfill the *hajj* is to make the world die within oneself and to turn one's life into Everlasting Life while still living in this world. This *hajj* is to make the world *(dunyā)* die in the world *(dunyā)* and for life to become Eternal (for *hayāt* to become *Hayāt).* To fulfill this is *hajj. Hajj* is to cut the connections of one's life, the connections to the base desires *(nafs)* and to the five elements. It is to cut the four

---

1. The affirmation of faith: *Lā ilāha ill-Allāh, Muhammadur-Rasūlullāh.* There is no god but God, and Muhammad is the Messenger of Allah. See also Appendix for the five *kalimahs.*

23

hundred trillion, ten thousand varieties of spiritual qualities and to establish with clarity that there is no Lord other than *Allāhu.*

The *dunyā* is made to die by the *dunyā.* The *dunyā* is this place where we live and all that we see. The *dunyā* within this *dunyā* is our body, our form *(sūrat).* The world within this body is made to die by the world. In this fifth *fard* of *hajj,* all the characteristics of the body, its thoughts, its intentions, and all such connections are made to die. This is how the world is made to die in the world and by the world, thereby making life Eternal *(Hayāt).*

Life, or *hayāt,* is the soul. This is within the body, and the world is also within the body. Within the outer world exists this body which is in itself a world, and within that body is the soul *(rūh)* which is life itself. We must make this soul eternal within the effulgence which is *Allāhu.* With that effulgence, the soul is made resplendent, and that resplendence becomes *Hayāt* (Eternal Life). The *hayāt* becomes *Hayāt.* Through the form *(sūrat)* of Allah's effulgence, through that light, the soul is made *Hayāt.* It is made resplendent. Through that light, life is surrendered to the One who is Eternal. We dedicate our *hayāt* to the One who is *Hayāt,* to *Allāhu ta'ālā,* Almighty God. When that state dawns, when one makes his world die to the outer world, when one makes his life resplend in the *Hayāt,* when one hands over all responsibility for that resplendent light of *hayāt* to the One who is *Hayāt*—only then is the fifth *fard* of *hajj* fulfilled.

Millions upon millions of people attempt to fulfill the *hajj.* But if one truly fulfills this state, the sound of Allah will resonate within. On that day, he will receive the wealth of Allah, His attributes, His actions, His three thousand gracious qualities, His ninety-nine powers *(wilāyāt)* and actions, the grace of divine knowledge *('ilm)*, the mercy of His grace, the grace of His qualities, the grace of faith, certitude, and determination *(īmān)*, the grace of love, the grace of wisdom, and all His undiminishing grace and mercy. On that day, one transforms his life into heaven, into God's kingdom. After completing the *hajj* of dying within Allah, one's life will be in heaven and not in hell. Even though one still has a body, life will be heaven. Even though one lives a life in this world, it will be a life filled with the grace of Allah. When one looks, it will be with Allah's resplendent gaze. When one listens, it will be with the ear that hears the sound of Allah. When one smells, he will smell the fragrance of Allah. When one speaks, it will be the speech of Allah. When one tastes, it will be the taste of Allah. One's actions of giving and receiving will be the actions of giving and receiving Allah's wealth. When one walks, one will be walking on Allah's path, focusing on Allah. One's heart will be Allah's heart, the throne of a true believer *('arshul-mu'min)*, a heart of light. All one's qualities will be the qualities and actions of Allah. Such is the state established by those who have fulfilled the fifth *fard* (obligatory duty) of *hajj*.

In that state, one considers all lives and creations as one's own. One knows and understands everything and gives peace to all creations. One understands all their sorrows and gives them love and comfort. One's life is a light that helps all creations in the world, showing them the tranquil path that can give peace, guiding them on the straight path of justice and integrity. One embraces all lives in one's heart, in unity. Such a one is a representative of Allah, His messenger, existing as His light and doing duty. Those who have attained this state have fulfilled the *fard* of *hajj*.

This is how the *hajj* must be fulfilled and completed. This completeness is *Īmān-Islām.* Whoever attains this state within has surely fulfilled the fifth *fard* of *hajj.* In truth, only one in a trillion truly fulfills this *fard.* Such a one will be living in heaven. This is why it is a very difficult matter to truly understand this fifth *fard* of *hajj.* Those who do not understand this consider it to be very easy, like a tourist's trip. Like sightseers traveling around the world, they perform the *hajj* and return home.

My love you, my brethren who were born with me. It is in the true state that Allah's *Rasūl* ﷺ fulfilled the *hajj* in the end. Having completed this duty, the *Rasūl* ﷺ said, "Allah has fulfilled my intentions. He has fulfilled His intention through me, and from now on, you must complete this *hajj* with unity." The *Rasūl* ﷺ said, "Finally, I am placing in your hands Allah's words. This is the completion of the *Qur'ān* and its meanings *(sabab).* This is the wealth that Allah has given. It is time for me to leave, to change. But I am placing in your hands Allah's words, actions, deeds, and wealth *(daulat).* If one understands this *Qur'ān* and fulfills this *hajj,* he will be in heaven. When he understands the *Qur'ān* fully, he will understand and fulfill the fifth *fard* of *hajj,* the most essential of the *furūd* (obligatory duties). That is *Īmān-Islām.*"

In the last stage, having finally fulfilled the *hajj* in this manner, the Noble Prophet, the *Rasūl* ﷺ, spoke these words. Those who have wisdom, who have the certitude of *īmān,* who have opened their hearts and looked within, who have understood divine knowledge *('ilm),* who have acquired God's qualities and understood, who act with Allah's actions, who have understood and received His attributes *(wilāyāt)* and His wealth will understand.

This is the fifth *fard* of *hajj* in *Īmān-Islām.* Whoever fulfills this *fard* of *hajj* will not live in this world or in the world within this world. The body is one world, and what we live in and see around us is another world. One is the realm of desire *(nafs)*, the soul *(rūh)*, elemental spirits *(rūhānī)*, and satanic thoughts and actions *(shaitāniyyat)* and the other is the physical world in which we live. Both these worlds must be made to die in us. We must make the world die by the world. After that, we will have Eternal Life *(Hayāt)* and dwell in heaven.

My children, creations born with me, my sons and daughters, you and we must think about how are we going to fulfill this fifth *fard*. When will we fulfill this *hajj*? When will we do this? When will we complete this? When will this inner death occur? When will we attain *Hayāt*? We must reflect on this. We must receive eternal life from the One who is Eternal and vanquish death by dying before death. We must understand, with certitude, how this can be accomplished. This is the *hajj* which we must understand. The fifth *fard* is very, very difficult to perform. The *Qur'ān* has not mentioned any *fard* beyond this. Why? When one has merged in Allah, what other duty is there for him? But as long as one has not disappeared in Allah, then one has not yet finished with the world and therefore has to perform these duties. These five *furūd* are essential, and human beings must fulfill them one by one. If one has completed them all, then one has disappeared and died within Allah and completed the *hajj*.

Life and death are in Allah's responsibility *(tawakkul)*. Bad and good *(sharr* and *khair)* are in His responsibility. Human beings must understand what good is and what evil is. On the Day of Reckoning *(Qiyāmah)*, Allah will make an inquiry. As long as the world is still present within oneself, there will be a questioning in the grave on the Day of

Reckoning and a judgment on Judgment Day. As long as the world is present within oneself, the questions will come. If one remains as the world within the world, there will be the questioning in the grave. When this world within the world exists, then there will be the questioning on the Day of Reckoning and a Judgment Day. Until one makes this world die by the world, and makes his life resplendent with *Hayāt,* one has not fulfilled the *hajj* of *Īmān-Islām.* This is the meaning of *hajj.*

You must understand what divine knowledge (*'ilm*) is. Allah is One who has so much wealth. His treasures will never diminish by even one atom. He holds the wealth of all three worlds in His hands. What will those who have received this wealth ever lack? It is certain that the wealth of the three worlds: the beginning (*awwal*), this world (*dunyā*), and the divine kingdom (*ākhirah*) are in His hands. Whatever wealth you are to receive in this world is in His hands. Whatever wealth you are to receive in the realm of the soul is in His hands. The wealth of the divine kingdom is in His hands. When one receives the wealth of the three worlds (*mubārakāt*), he will realize completeness. If a human being understands the five *furūd* and fulfills the fifth *fard* of *hajj,* then what want will he have? Nothing will be lacking. He will be fulfilled. But as long as one does not fulfill this *hajj,* then there will always be deficiencies in one's life and in one's prayer, in one's worship, devotions, thoughts, and intentions, in one's gaze, in one's sound, in one's mind and qualities, in one's speech and taste. It is certain that something will always be lacking in one's body and in one's actions of giving and receiving. In that state; human beings will always experience a wealth that is deficient, a happiness that is incomplete. They will never be fulfilled or complete.

On the path of wisdom, we must open divine knowledge
(*'ilm*) and wisdom, with absolute certitude, resolution, and
the strength of *īmān*. We must contemplate and understand
the wealth of Allah which is His qualities and His actions.
When we understand this divine knowledge with unity,
love, generosity, correct conduct and behavior, with prayer,
paying obeisance at His feet, prostrating *(sajdah)* and bow-
ing *(rukū')* before Him, praising Him, surrendering to Him
(tawakkul), and merging with Him; when *īmān* is strongly
established and wisdom dawns; when we understand divine
knowledge and His qualities fill us, then we will understand
the secret—that good and evil *(khair* and *sharr)* are in Allah's
trust *(tawakkul).* We will understand the essence and the
manifestation *(dhāt* and *sifāt).* We will understand what is
permissible and impermissible *(halāl* and *harām).* We will
understand heaven and hell. We will be able to understand
this world and the divine world *(dunyā* and *ākhirah).* We will
be able to understand the soul and the elemental spirit *(rūh*
and *rūhānī).* We will be able to understand the base desires
(nafs ammārah), truth, and goodness. We can understand
hatred and love, truth and falsehood. We can understand
what love is, what wisdom is, and what lack of wisdom is.
With that divine knowledge, we will be able to understand
all this. Only when Allah's qualities and that divine knowledge are complete within us and when we have fulfilled this
hajj will we receive His wealth and heaven. Our death will
be overcome, and our life will be Eternal *(Hayāt)* in this
world and in the divine world. We must understand this
with certainty.

Our *Rasūl,* the Noble Prophet ﷺ, completed this fifth *fard*
of *hajj.* He made the world within him die; he made the
world within the world die. He died while still being alive.

He completed and fulfilled this *hajj*. Then he placed in our hands the treasure and the wealth that had to be given to us. Whatever treasures Allah gave to him, he gave to us. He taught and displayed *īmān*. He taught and exhibited wisdom. He explained and revealed divine knowledge *('ilm)*. He explained and demonstrated Allah's qualities and gave witness to the nature of Allah. Before he left the world, he related, "This is a treasure which never perishes. Through this, you should correct your life in the proper way and establish a direct path between you and Him." The Prophet ﷺ taught the unity that all of Adam's children are one family forever, that there is one God and one prayer. To pray to Him is true prayer. He is a treasure without equal, parallel, or comparison. That is the One power—Allah. Every prophet brought this one point. They brought this one treasure so that we could understand its secret.

The Prophet ﷺ said, "All this was gathered together, and I have brought it in completeness. Allah gave this to me and told me to communicate it to all. Now I have explained it to you." The *Qur'ān*, God's word *(kalām)* that was brought, is divine knowledge, the *Tiru Qur'ān*.[2] Buried within this are all the words and actions of all the prophets, words which Allah told them to speak. Analyze each word. Understand, know, and accept each word. With certitude, you must realize that all are children of Adam ﷺ. Allah is the only One. He is the only Lord worthy of worship. Understand the five *furūd*. Understand the final *hajj*. That is the correct way of performing the pilgrimage. This is the meaning of *hajj*.

My love you, my grandchildren, my daughters, sons, my brothers, sisters. Each of us should reflect. You must under-

---

2. The original *Qur'ān;* the inner *Qur'ān* inscribed within the heart.

stand how to fulfill this fifth *fard* of *hajj* and then try to complete it. You must live in love and unity, understanding that we are all one family. Living as one, praying and surrendering to that One alone is how we can become *Īmān-Islām*. To understand the five *furūd* (obligatory duties) is *Īmān-Islām*. That which brings fruition to *Īmān-Islām* is the *kalimah;* that which understands it is wisdom; that which brings clarity to wisdom is the qualities, and the light of those qualities is Allah. We must understand this.

My love you, my grandchildren. Every child must strive to do this. This fifth *fard* (obligatory duty) is extremely difficult. The other four are easy. They can be done. But to have faith in God, to pray to Him, to establish a direct connection with Him, and to complete the *hajj* within Him is difficult. These two, prayer and *hajj,* are difficult. To connect these two with Allah and bring them to completion is difficult. You must think about this.

My love you. May Allah grant you the straight path of His grace and His *'ilm,* so that you may accomplish this. May He grant you faith, *īmān,* and the qualities of His wisdom. May He grant you His grace. May He lengthen the life *(hayāt)* that He has given you. May He help you to victoriously complete the tasks you have come here to perform. *Āmīn.* May Allah help you to fulfill this exalted *fard,* the fifth *fard* of *hajj,* to receive the complete treasure, and to make your *hayāt* into *Hayāt* and to make it resplend. *Āmīn.* You must try.

May the peace and grace and blessings of Allah be upon you. *As-salāmu 'alaikum wa rahmatullāhi wa barakātuhu. Āmīn.*

September 28, 1982

3
The Five Duties of Īmān-Islām

QUESTIONER: I don't know if I should go on *hajj* now or when I get older.

BAWA MUHAIYADDEEN: Your intention to go on *hajj* is good. There are five *furūd* (obligatory duties) in *Īmān-Islām*. There are the five and the six principles.[1] *Hajj* is the final *fard*.

The state of *hajj* is the state of death. That is the state in which you must fulfill the *hajj*. One must not go on *hajj* just to earn the title of *"Hajjiyar."*[2] *Allāhu ta'ālā Nāyan* (the Lord, God Almighty) in His glory revealed these duties to Muhammad *Mustafar-Rasūl* (the Chosen Messenger ﷺ). Allah has three mouths—*alif, lām,* and *mīm*.[3] With a blossoming

---

1. The five *furūd* (sing. *fard*) refer to the five pillars of Islam: *ash-shahādah* (witnessing that there is no god but God, and Muhammad is the Messenger of God), prayer, charity, fasting, and holy pilgrimage *(hajj)*.

Allah has also given us six inner *furūd,* which the Sufis have explained. 1) If you go deep into Allah with the certitude of unwavering faith, you will see that within this eye of yours is an inner eye which can gaze upon Allah. 2) Within this nostril is a piece of flesh which can smell the fragrance of Allah. 3) Within this ear is a piece of flesh which can hear the sounds of Allah. 4) Within this tongue is a piece of flesh which can taste the beauty and the divine knowledge of Allah and know the taste of His wealth. 5) Within this tongue is also a voice which converses with Him and recites His remembrance in a state of total absorption. 6) And within this innermost heart is a piece of flesh where the eighteen thousand universes, the heavens, and His kingdom are found. And there the angels, the heavenly beings, prophets, and lights of Allah prostrate before Him.

2. A title used in Sri Lanka for someone who has gone on the holy pilgrimage more than once.

3. Bawa Muhaiyaddeen ﷺ explains that these three Arabic letters represent the Triple Flame, the Triple Effulgence, the true form of man. *Alif* (l) is Allah,

35

heart, He showered the teachings of grace upon the *Rasūl* (ﷺ) through these three mouths. In that teaching, primary importance was given to the five *furūd*.

The first *fard* (obligatory duty) to have faith and certitude in Allah. It is to know and accept Him without any doubt, wavering, or selfish envy *(hasad)*. It is to accept that God is One and has no equal. There is no god equal to Him. Allah alone is God, the *Rabb* (the Lord). You should know this with certitude and accept Him.

Second, having accepted that He is such a Creator, we must worship and glorify God with *īmān* (unshakable faith) and a melting heart. We must accept that there is no one worthy of worship except *Allāhu ta'ālā* and give the full responsibility of our heart to Him. We must accept God alone as our wealth and grace. God alone is our paradise *(firdaus)*. He is the Mercy and Compassion of all the universes *(Rahmatul-'ālamīn)*. He is the wealth for the three worlds: the beginning *(awwal)*, this world *(dunyā)*, and the hereafter *(ākhirah)*. We must accept God with firm certitude and worship and glorify Him. These are the first two *furūd* in *Īmān-Islām*. First is to have firm faith, and second is to worship and glorify Him.

The third *fard* is charity. God is the only wealth. Therefore, we must realize that we do not have any other wealth. In *Īmān-Islām*, Allah is our only wealth. We must give full

---

the Creator. *Lām* (ل) is the *Nūr*, the light of wisdom. And *mīm* (م) is Muhammad (ﷺ) (the created manifestation, the light of the soul). Who are you? You are Muhammad (ﷺ). What is inside you? The light, the *lām*. That is wisdom. What is within that? God, the *alif*, who is without sound. All three are joined together in one form, the body; within the body is the light, and within the light is the mystery. This is the explanation of the relationship between the *Rabb*, the Creator, and *insān*, the created being. (From *Questions of Life—Answers of Wisdom*, page 264.)

responsibility to Him alone. No matter what happens, a person in that state of faith will have patience *(sabūr)*. Patience is the preface to *Īmān-Islām*. Second, such a person will have contentment *(shakūr)*. Third, for whatever nourishment he receives at any given moment, he will have contentment and praise God saying, *"Al-hamdu lillāh!"* Whether he receives a rich meal of *buriyani* (a traditional rice dish) or only a drink of water, he will say, *"Al-hamdu lillāh. We accept You."* Fourth, for what is to occur the next moment he will surrender to God, saying, *"Tawakkul-ʿalallāh. It is in Your hands, O God."*

For what is to happen at this moment, we say, *"Al-hamdu lillāh. All praise is to God! We accept this as sufficient."* In the next moment, we may be alive or we may be dead, but for whatever is to happen we surrender to God, saying, *"Tawakkul-ʿalallāh."* This the introduction to *Īmān-Islām*. If we attain this state and see Allah alone as our only wealth, then the One who performs the duty and the One who receives it will be Allah. *Khair* and *sharr* (good and evil) are in Allah's trust *(tawakkul)*. Allah is responsible for the *dhāt* and *sifāt*. The *dhāt* is grace and the *sifāt* is all that is created. We must also understand what food is *halāl* and what food is *harām*. *Halāl* is what is allowed, and *harām* is what is forbidden. Once you understand that, you are in the state of *Īmān-Islām*.

Īmān is Islam. If there is no *īmān,* there is no Islam. We are all children of Adam ﷺ. Everyone is in Islam. God created human beings with the twenty-eight letters, which include the *alif, lām,* and *mīm.*[4] Therefore, all of everything is in Islam. Allah created life *(hayāt)* with purity. The person

---

4. This refers to the twenty-eight letters of the Arabic alphabet. Each section of the human form is represented by one of these letters. When man purifies

who realizes Allah without any doubt, who accepts Allah alone and worships Him, that person is in *Īmān-Islām. Īmān* is Islam. If one does not have *īmān,* he will not be Islam. We must understand this.

Allāhu ta'ālā Nāyan revealed this to Muhammad *Mustafar-Rasūl* ⊙, through His three mouths of *alif, lām,* and *mīm.* The *alif* which is Allah resonates with sound. The letters *alif, lām,* and *mīm* are given various sounds according to their diacritical marks. If the mark is placed on the top of a letter, it gives one sound; if it is below, it gives another. In Arabic, the seven diacritical marks create different sounds. The letters by themselves have no sound. We have to give the sound. The *Qur'ān* exists without sound. We give it the sound. *Īmān* and wisdom must give it sound. Then Allah's resonance can be heard. Only if we give it sound will He hear. Otherwise it is silent *(ummī).* It is just there. We must understand this. There are seven instruments. These are the seven states of consciousness: feeling, awareness, intellect, judgment, subtle wisdom, divine analytic wisdom which is the wisdom of the *Qutb,* and divine luminous wisdom which is the wisdom of light, the *lām,* the *Nūr, Nūr Muhammad Mustafā.* With these seven we must give it the sound of wisdom. Then Allah will hear it. This is the *Ummul-Qur'ān,* the inner *Qur'ān* of a human being *(insān). Insān-Qur'ān.* This is the *Sūratul-Fātihah.*[5] *Al-hamdu lillāh,* all praise is to God. Understand this.

When we give the sound through these instruments,

_____

himself, these letters take the form of light and appear as the *Ummul-Qur'ān* or the eternal source of the *Qur'ān* revealed to Muhammad ⊙.

5. Literally, the opening chapter of the *Qur'ān* recited at the beginning of every prayer. But here it refers to the inner form of man; the clarity of understanding the four elements of the body (earth, fire, water, and air), and the realization of the self and Allah within.

Allāhu ta'ālā Nāyan hears us, listens to us, understands us, speaks to us, and gives us His grace *(rahmat)*. But because we did not understand this, when Muhammad *Mustafar-Rasūl* 🕊 went on the *Mi'rāj*,[6] out of his compassionate grace, he pleaded with Allah to make it easier for us by reducing the fifty-one times of prayer to five. We must understand these five times of prayer *(waqts)*. These are the *furūd* (obligatory duties) and they are important.

First is the early morning prayer *(subh)*. During that prayer, we must understand the section of the earth within us, the one fistful of earth. We must understand this section, making it die and extracting the essence. Second is the noon-time prayer *(zuhr)*. During that prayer, we need to understand the section of fire within us and make it die. This is the section of satan, which includes the qualities of anger, arrogance, the possessiveness of mine, yours, 'I', and 'you'. Third is the afternoon prayer *('asr)*, the section of water. It relates to creation, to lust, resentment, passion, envy, miserliness, bigotry, arrogance, *karma,* and *māyā.* All these are connected to creation. We must sever these connections. That is the time of *'asr.*

Next is the sunset prayer *(maghrib)*. This is when day and night, old age and death must be made to die. Fifth is the evening prayer, *'ishā'. Hayāt-maut.* Life-death. We must make the connection to the world, to birth and to darkness, die. After making these die, we must join with *Allāhu ta'ālā Nāyan* in the realm of the soul.

Beyond that is the state of *sūfiyyat* or the realm of divine knowledge *('ilm)*. In that state there is no time *(waqt)*, no day or night. In *sūfiyyat*, one speaks without speaking, worships

---

6. The mystical journey of Prophet Muhammad 🕊 through the heavens, during which the divine decree of the five-times prayer was given.

without worshiping, sleeps without sleeping, eats without
eating, and dies without dying. Such a one constantly glorifies God and has no set time of prayer. He performs 43,242
bows and prostrations *(rukū' and sajdah)* to God in a day.[7]
That is the state of *sūfiyyat.* There are the five times of prayer,
and then there is the sixth, when one dies in the glorification
of God *(tasbīh).* That is *sūfiyyat.* To one in that state, the
world will be forbidden *(harām).* Everything in the world
will be forbidden, and Allah alone will be permissible *(halāl).*
These are the important inner meanings of *Īmān-Islām.*

Because we have not understood this, we hold onto the
desires for earth, gold, wealth, and woman. We cling onto
the seven base desires *(nafs ammārah). Allāhu ta'ālā Nāyan*
created the sun, the moon, the earth, water, air, fire, and ether
as common to all. God provided a place for each one of His
creations. For those that dwell in trees, He provided a place
in the trees. For those that dwell in burrows, He provided a
place in the burrows. For those that live in anthills, He gave
anthills. For those who live in the jungle, He gave a place in
the jungle. For those who live in caves, He provided a place
in caves. God has given a suitable place to the crawling ants,
worms, insects, and leeches, every creation. For those that
dwell in the air, He provided a space in the air. For those that
dwell in the water, He provided a place there. For those that
live on the earth, He provided a place there. For those that dwell
in the fire, He provided a place there. For those that live in the
ether, He provided a place there. Allah, the Lord *(Rabb),* has
given His common property to His entire creation.

All creations are given freedom and a place to live. They
are all given water, air, fire, and a connection to earth and

---

7. Bawa Muhaiyaddeen calculates that man takes 43,242 breaths, inhalations
and exhalations, each day. Therefore, one in this state prays with every breath.

ether. But man grabs for himself what Allah has created as common to all. He snatches the homes of others for himself. He claims the water as his own. He claims the air as his own. He makes the sun his own. He makes the earth his own. He claims the moon is his. He attempts to make what was common to all his private property. This is the cause of all the battles and wars.

It is because of this that God sent the *Rasūl* (ﷺ). God said, "The children of My Adam are fighting over this common property, and they are perishing. Allah is One. Man can have only Me as his property. Everything else is common to all." To make mankind realize this, God sent the 124,000 prophets, the lights of God, those with divine wisdom *(qutbs),* and the saints *(auliyā')* as witnesses to prove that Allah is One. Out of these 124,000 prophets, God selected eight special prophets: Adam, Noah, Abraham, Ishmael, Moses, David, Jesus, and Muhammad (may the peace and blessings of Allah be upon them all). There are twenty-five prophets spoken of in the *Qur'ān,* and from those twenty-five, God selected eight prophets as special. To the last of the eight prophets, God said, "Yā Muhammad, go and tell the people that all of this belongs to Me. It is common property. No one owns it. Tell your followers that I said this." Allah revealed the 6,666 verses and countless numbers of direct communications *(ahādīth)* to Muhammad (ﷺ). The followers of Allah's *Rasūl* (ﷺ) accepted these. But very few of them accepted Allah alone as their property, rejecting everything else. Those who did were rejected by the world. Some were killed, some were tortured, and some were driven out of their homeland. They left their homes behind, giving all responsibility to God.

In the end, *Allāhu ta'ālā Nāyan* gave these words as proof to Muhammad *Mustafar-Rasūl* (ﷺ) and told him to explain these five duties. "This is *Īmān-Islām*. People do not realize that I, alone, am the permanent property, the Absolute One, who has no equal, who can never be destroyed, the undiminishing One, the One who never dies, the One who comforts and gives according to the needs of each heart, the Creator and the Nourisher, the One who gives the soul *(rūh)* and then calls it back again, the One who gives judgment and then gives the place appropriate to each one's striving.

"I am the One who does all this. They have forgotten Me, *Yā Rasūlullāh*. I have given you the name *Rahmatul-'ālamīn* (the Mercy of all the universes). Go, *Yā Rasūl,* and tell this to your followers. To those who are in the state of *Īmān-Islām,* to those who realize Me, the things and the gifts of the world will be forbidden *(harām)*. If they realize Me, these are forbidden. Tell your people not to accept these gifts from the world. Everything belongs to Me, and for those who accept Me, these things are forbidden. It is forbidden for someone to give what belongs to Me without My permission. It is I alone who must give and I alone who must receive." So said *Allāhu ta'ālā Nāyan* (the Lord, God Almighty).

We who have not realized this say, "We have *īmān!* We are in *Īmān-Islām!*" But we have forgotten the words of God and have given great value to earth, gold, and woman. *Allāhu ta'ālā* sent Muhammad, the *Rasūl* 🕊, as the final Prophet to explain, to make us understand, and to cut this section. But no matter what the *Rasūl* 🕊 said, we did not accept it. We still had our attachments. During the time of the Prophet 🕊, people were following satan and making statues of countless numbers of gods. They made innumerable idols of animals. They made snakes, scorpions, crows, eagles, fish, cats, rats, dogs, foxes, lions, tigers, and satans into gods. There were 330 million idols in the *Ka'bah* and forty-eight thousand smaller statues as well. The people kept all these in the *Ka'bah* and worshiped them. Some of these idols were destroyed by Prophet Abraham ☾, some by Prophet Moses ☾, and some by other prophets. In those days, satan used to speak to people from the statues and so did ghosts. After the *Rasūl* ☾ came, the mouths of all those idols were sealed. All the idols and their miracles were shattered. They fell face down in the *Ka'bah* and shattered.

The *Rasūl* ☾ gave witness that Allah alone exists. But because the people did not accept this in the right way, God ordained the five *furūd*, the five-times prayer. Just as small children are taught step by step, the people were given these prayers as an easy method to strengthen their *īmān*. People could at least do this. Those who have *īmān* must understand this. The five *furūd* were obligatory for those people who could not understand the deeper meanings. The deeper meanings I spoke of earlier are for those who have absolute *īmān*. For them, Allah is the only wealth. Within the five times of prayer, they must cut the connection to the five elements of earth, fire, water, air, and ether. These five should be made to die. This is the inner meaning of the five-times prayer. This is the Sufism of *Īmān-Islām*. Because people did not attain this state, the five principles were sent to help them realize it gradually. The first is to have faith in Allah, second is to worship Allah alone, third is to give charity, fourth is fasting, and fifth is *hajj*. These were given so that people could progress gradually. We have to understand this.

If we have that *īmān* which accepts Allah and keeps Him as our grace, then no other wealth will exist for us. We must understand this with faith and *īmān*. Those who have *īmān* must only possess that which they can return to Allah. All that we cannot bring back to Allah is *harām* (forbidden) to us, and we cannot keep it. We cannot take the earth with us; it is a common property belonging to the earth. We cannot take water; that belongs to the water. We cannot bring air or fire. All these are forbidden. We cannot bring our base desires *(nafs)*. These are *harām*. Things that cannot be returned to Allah are forbidden. Those with *īmān* cannot accept any of these as gifts.

If one reflects on this, he would realize that the giving and receiving of gifts is *harām*. If a person has only Allah, how can he give or receive anything? His wealth is Allah alone. What can he give or receive? This is one of the things we have to understand in the ocean of divine knowledge *(bahrul-'ilm)*. For those who do not understand this and act accordingly, fasting was ordained so that they might at least realize the hunger of others. While fasting a person must look at himself and observe how tired he becomes when hungry and how his body loses strength and weight. Let him realize this, so that he will share what he has with others. At least man must realize this and help his brethren.

Next, God said a person should give in charity at least five or ten percent of what he has earned in order to help others. But man did not do so. He forgot that duty, too. People would even steal for their own gain. Finally, God ordained *hajj* as the fifth duty. Give away everything you have and go to Mecca and Medina wearing the pilgrim's shroud *(ihrām)*. Give your wife the dowry *(mahr)* that is due her. Give what must be given to your children. Give what must be given to the poor and your neighbors. Keep Allah alone with you as your wealth and make this journey of *hajj*. Wear your shroud when you go on *hajj*, because at that stage the world is dead to you.

Go and surrender to God in that state of death. Place all

responsibility in His hands and fulfill this fifth duty of *hajj*. Go and die in Allah. Be born again within Him, and from within Him become Muhammad ﷺ. The meaning of Muhammad ﷺ is the beauty and the light of Allah. Receive that light and beauty. Surrender yourselves in Allah. Be born again in Allah and do duty from within Him. That is *hajj*. That is the inner *fard*. These are the five principles out of the five and six *furūd* decreed for us in *Īmān-Islām*. If we can complete the *hajj* and die in this state, then our *hajj* will be fulfilled. Otherwise, we simply go to Mecca as tourists. Christians go to Rome as tourists. Other religions have various places of worship to which they go as tourists. Those who go on *hajj* bring back titles like *"Hajjiyar."* Once you truly finish this obligation, there is no other *fard* (duty). There are only five *furūd* (obligatory duties). Once in your lifetime you must fulfill the *hajj*. A person must die to the world. That is *hajj*. If one fulfills these *furūd*, then he is in *Īmān-Islām*. This is the true way.

Man must understand the duties of *Īmān-Islām*. The *hajj* that is practiced today is simply a tourist's trip. People leave home saying, *"Labbaik...labbaik. I am here...I am here...."*[8] They go on *hajj*, and they buy gold, silver rings, vessels, and radios to bring back home. When they return, they think they have completed the *hajj*, that the *furūd* have been completed and now they can do anything they want. *Hajj* is only done once in a lifetime! Once that is finished, what more is there to do? Instead, people return home and start erecting billboards for hell. This is what is happening in the world today.

The *Rasūl* ﷺ performed a different *hajj*. The *hajj* per-

---

8. See Appendix for further explanation.

formed 1,200 to 1,300 years ago by those with *īmān* was as we described earlier. That is the way the Sufis did it at that time. But the *hajj* of today is like a tourist trip to Mecca and Medina. It is important to understand the true *hajj* and to do it in that manner. Just because you go to Mecca, circum-ambulate the *Ka'bah,* and pray there, will Allah give you heaven? No. You must think about this. Did all the camels, cats, and dogs that lived there, and even Abū Jahl and his son, 'Ikrimah,[9] and his children, and all the other people born in Mecca attain heaven?

If you can go with faith and *īmān* and fulfill the *hajj* in the way that it should be done, that is good. That is what this fool thinks. Nowadays, people go to Mecca in a casual way, yet they think they have fulfilled this *fard* (obligatory duty) of *hajj.* I do not know anything about that. They call it a *fard,* but the inner meaning is as I have just explained.

Everything has an inner and an outer meaning. The outer is the body and the inner is the heart *(qalb).* Deeper than that is the essence *(dhāt).* Many, many levels can be found there. Within that is *īmān.* Deeper within that is the light of *Nūr Muhammad.* Deeper within that are the qualities of that light, and deeper within that is the resplendent wisdom of *Nūr Muhammad.* And within the realm of that wisdom, the sound of Allah resonates. His grace radiates there. The judgment of His kingdom is understood there. If we die before reaching that place, we will die as unbelievers *(kāfirs).* But if we can reach that state, we will die in *Īmān-Islām.*

---

9. Abū Jahl: One of the foremost enemies of Muhammad ﷺ. His real name was 'Amir ibn Misham, but the Muslims nicknamed him Abū Jahl, or "The Father of Ignorance." 'Ikrimah: The son of Abū Jahl who for many years was a determined opponent of Muhammad ﷺ but later embraced Islam and became a companion of the Prophet ﷺ.

There are seventy-three groups.[10] One who reaches that final state will die as a *mu'min,* a true believer. Those who do not will die as *kāfirs.* We must understand this during our lifetime, before we die. Think about this.

Therefore my brother, you are young. Others are going, and if you, too, would like to go, then go and come. I cannot stop you. But you must understand. All right? *As-salāmu 'alaikum wa rahmatullāhi wa barakātuhu kulluhu.* May the peace, the beneficence, and the blessings of God be with you.

September 11, 1980

---

10. Bawa Muhaiyaddeen ☺ frequently refers to the seventy-three groups of human beings. Only the seventy-third group consists of true human beings with perfect faith. Of the other seventy-three groups, seventy have no faith in God and the remaining two have faith, but they also still have a desire for the world and its pleasures. (From *Islam and World Peace: Explanations of a Sufi,* page 57.)

4
The Meaning of the Ka'bah

QUESTION: What is the significance of the *Ka'bah?*

BAWA MUHAIYADDEEN: We in Islam still do not understand this. The Prophet Abraham ﷺ built a mosque on earth as an example and called it the *Ka'bah.* The *Rasūl* ﷺ came later and repaired this same mosque which had been destroyed after the time of Abraham ﷺ. This is the *Ka'bah.* What you asked about is a big question. This is a very important matter that Islam has not fully understood.

During the time of the *Rasūl* ﷺ, the *Ka'bah* was rebuilt. The *Rasūl* ﷺ proclaimed, "Come! Gather together here." It is said that the *Ka'bah* is the central point for the world. Whatever a man considers as the focal point of his life is his *Ka'bah.* If with his *īmān* (unshakable faith) and certitude he sees *Allāhu* as the Complete One, then wherever he sees that Completeness, that is the *Ka'bah.* Wherever he prays to Him, that is the *Ka'bah.* Wherever he has this *īmān* and this connection, that is the *Ka'bah.*

Abraham ﷺ constructed this building and revealed it as a place for the remembrance of Allah. But it is only an outward example. Wherever those who are in *Īmān-Islām,* in purity, congregate—that is the *Ka'bah.* Wherever everyone gathers in unity as one—that is the *Ka'bah.* Any place that satan cannot approach—that is the *Ka'bah.* Where Allah and purity and His *qudrat* (power) are together in one place— that is the *Ka'bah.* That place which is formed with Allah's three thousand gracious attributes and His ninety-nine

beautiful qualities *(wilāyāt)* is the *Ka'bah*. When there is
unity in the three worlds *(awwal, dunyā,* and *ākhirah)*—that
is Islam. Then there will be Islam in the beginning *(awwal)*,
Islam in this world *(dunyā)*, and Islam in the divine kingdom
(ākhirah). That is Islam. The place where you join in unity
with Allah in all three worlds is the *Ka'bah*. That is the
throne of God *('arsh)*. It is a place of worship and prayer. It
is paradise *(firdaus)*. Such a place is called the *Ka'bah*.

No matter where you are, the place where you unite with
Allah is the *Ka'bah*. When you focus upon the place of union
between you and Allah within your heart, that place of purity is the *Ka'bah*. That will be the West.[1] We were born in
one place and must travel to the other. One place is where
the light was sent to us, and the other is where it disappears.
Allah sent this light, this soul to us. We must take it back,
give it into His responsibility, and disappear within Him.
The place where our soul and our *īmān* are taken back and
absorbed into Allah is the *Ka'bah*. The place where our
prayer unites with Him is the *Ka'bah*. That is the place of
worship for *Īmān-Islām*, and that place is within the *qalb* (innermost heart).

Within the *qalb* is the station of *īmān* where we recite
the *kalimah: Lā ilāha ill-Allāh, Muhammadur-Rasūlullāh,
sallallāhu 'alaihi wa sallam.* (There is no god but God, and
Muhammad is the Messenger of God. May the peace and

---

1. In Islam, when you pray, you must face toward the West, toward the
qiblah. According to the Sufi explanation, one is born in the East. Man's creation
is in the East. That is where he appears. And what is the West? That is the
place where he disappears, where he finishes. He appears in the East and
disappears in the West. This is what is really meant when Islam says, "Face
toward the West." He must disappear in his prayer. Since he was born in the
East, he must lose himself and die in the West, die in his prayer. The West is
the final state where he loses himself in God. (From a discourse given on
February 1, 1975.)

blessings of God be upon him). That is where we speak to Allah with this *kalimah* and with our love for the *Rasūl* ﷺ. This is the *Mi'rāj* (Muhammad's mystical journey to meet God). That place where the Prophet ﷺ conversed with Allah is called the *Ka'bah,* and the place where we converse with Allah is also called the *Ka'bah.* Where our soul, our *īmān,* and our purity converse with Allah, that place is called the *Ka'bah.* The pure *qalb* is called the *Ka'bah.* Perfectly pure places are called the *Ka'bah.* The place where you perform perfectly pure worship and prayer is the *Ka'bah.*

There are many meanings to this. It is Allah's secret *(sirr).* In Islam, the place where everything unites as one is the *Ka'bah.* This is a place where there is no separation in all three worlds, in the beginning *(awwal),* this world *(dunyā),* or in the divine kingdom *(ākhirah).* That is where there are no differences and where we meet Allah and the *Rasūl* ﷺ. There are three stations: the *qalb,* the *'arsh,* and the *kursī.*[2] *The qalb* one-pointedly focuses upon the *'arsh,* and then the *kursī* bows down and prostrates *(rukū'* and *sajdah)* within Allah. The *kursī* glorifies Allah *(tasbīh)* and surrenders. With love in the heart and knowing Allah, one's wisdom and *īmān* surrender to Him. The place where the *kursī* touches Allah, that is the *Ka'bah.*

When one has this one-pointedness and performs every prayer *(waqt)* in this manner, then the *Ka'bah* is within him. This is the *Ka'bah* on the inside. On the outside, when you face the *qiblah,*[3] in a mosque, the *mihrāb*[4] is in front of you.

---

2. *'arsh*—The throne of God; the plenitude from which God rules; the station located on the crown of the head.

3. *qiblah*—The direction one faces in prayer. Internally, it is the throne of God within the heart *(qalb).*

4. *mihrāb* (A) Literally, *mihrāb* is the prayer niche in the front of the mosque indicating the direction of Mecca. The third verb form derived from the same

Mihrāb means the battlefield, a place where you fight. When true prayer is done, the *Ka'bah* is the *qiblah*. The outer places of worship are the battlefields where we must join together to fight the things within us. We have to fight the evil qualities within us. We must conquer them all, cut them away, be victorious, and glorify Allah *(tasbīh)*. We must be victorious, conquering all these. This is what is done in the mosques when we face the *mihrāb,* the battlefield. First, we must fight and gain victory here and then go to the *Ka'bah* to pray. That is where we all unite as one, in Islam, in that place where there are no differences. That is the *Ka'bah*.

The ones who pray in that *Ka'bah* will never see hell. They will not be questioned on Judgment Day. They will not be questioned. They have communed with Allah. With every breath, they bow down *(rukū')* to His wealth *(daulat)*. In this world and the hereafter, they are Allah's witnesses, testifying that Allah exists. They are the ones who prove the existence of Allah. The place where they worship is the *Ka'bah*.

The *Ka'bah* is where you surrender to Him with your *īmān*. Once you have become victorious in the battles against your evil qualities, having cut away everything else, and you realize that Allah alone exists—then that is Islam. When you pray in that state, that is the *Ka'bah*. Then there is no battlefield, no *mihrāb*. It is a place of worship. Then it is truly the *Ka'bah*. All praise is to God *(al-hamdu lillāh)*. Do you understand?

QUESTIONER: Yes.

September 5, 1983

---

root means to wage war. Thus, the *mihrāb* is the point of focus which is the instrument in waging the inner war against that which is other than Allah.

5
Circling the Open Heart

O God, Allah, *a'ūdhu billāhi minash-shaitānir-rajīm*. (I seek refuge in God from the evils of satan.) *Bismillāhir-Rahmānir-Rahīm*. (In the name of God, Most Merciful, Most Compassionate.) May all praise, praising, and blessings belong to You forever. *Āmīn*. May You bless us with Your grace and Your qualities. You are the Unfathomable Ruler of grace, the One who is incomparable love, the One of plenitude who gives us the undiminishing wealth of grace. You are the Greatest Emperor *(Badushāh)* of both worlds, the One who bestows the three tasty fruits of sweetness, milk, and honey to my heart. You are the Light to my wisdom. You are the One who is the Soul to my soul, the Causal One for all of my actions. You reveal this life and the next life, night and day. You reveal this life as light and the next life as darkness. You reveal it within me and give that explanation daily, day and night, at every moment. In this life, You make my time of wisdom the daytime of divine wisdom *(gnānam)* and make my time of ignorance the nighttime of ignorance and desire in hell. You provide the explanation of these two. You have given an explanation of so much within us.

O Father of the soul who resonates, existing as Wisdom within wisdom, You are the Soul to the soul, beyond the beginningless beginning and the primal beginning *(anāthi and āthi)*. O God, You exist beyond everything, always resonating, as the original treasure. You are the One Supreme

Being, *ill-Allāh*. You are the Solitary One, the One who rules alone, the One without comparison, the One without parallel, the Lone One, without anyone and without the six evils. You have no one: no relations, no relationships, no attachments. You do not have the six evils of lust, hatred, fanaticism, envy, greed, and attachment. You do not have the thought that someone will come to protect You, not today, tomorrow, or any day. You exist always as Truth within truth. You are the only One who is a Father and King to all of everything. You are God.

You are the One who provides food and water for every moving creature, the One who provides nourishment. You are the Giver, the Taker, the Beckoner, and the Creator. You are the Ruler, the Emperor to all lives. You are eternally good. You are forever doing good. You are the One with no evil or evil actions whatsoever. You have only the qualities of goodness. You are the One who has discarded the harvest and the actions that are evil. O One of grace to all lives, You are God, the First, the Supreme Being. May You grant us Your grace by giving us Your good thoughts, wisdom, and actions. *Āmīn. Āmīn.*

May You drive away all our sins, dispel our sorrows and all the evils which surround us: the inherent evils of birth, the inherent evils of *karma,* and the flaws that come from our thoughts and intentions. Sins rolled and gathered together and became the embryo which became a form, a fistful of earth of this world. That earth of the world grew by consuming the earth. *Karma* grew by consuming *karma,* the flesh grew by consuming flesh, water grew by consuming water, fire grew by consuming fire, and air grew by consuming air. In this way, man devoured man, satan devoured satan, demons devoured demons. One quality devoured another

The five kalimahs, God, and prayer are the seven tawāfs. For a true human being, insān, these seven joined together are like a mendicant's large pouch. The innermost heart (qalb) is such a pouch. Within this pouch exists the wisdom known as the qutbiyyat.

—M. R. BAWA MUHAIYADDEEN

quality, and all together they formed this body. This body is a body of sin, a body of *karma,* a body of hell. It is burdened by sins and flaws. You, who are the great Soul, the great Father in the great realm, God, the Almighty Lord *(Allāhu ta'ālā Nāyan),* the Merciful One *(Rahmān),* the Lord of the universes, the One who bestows His grace, the One who is patient, the One who is Divine Patience *(Sabūr),* You are our Father. You are the Supreme One, the Supreme Realm, the Supreme Deity. You are without form or shape.

On the day that I understand how to realize You, then I will be able to see You. If I see myself, then I can see You within me. This is true wisdom. I must know this with absolute certainty. O Allah, one who does not see the well cannot draw water. One who does not see the earth cannot dig a well to quench one's thirst. It is not enough to merely look at the earth. Only if one digs can one obtain water.

Similarly, we each must know, "Who am I?" I must know who I am. I have to realize the path I am on and recognize whether I am a man, a beast, or a satan. If I see that I am a satan, then that aspect and those qualities of satan must be discarded. If I see that I am an animal, then that aspect has to be discarded. And, if I am a human being, then I must hold onto that section of being truly human and understand it within myself. Only when we understand this can we know who we truly are. Once we have discovered this, then we have to reach beyond. We each have to see, "What is within me?" We must sift within ourselves. We have to dig and see what lies within ourselves. We must look for the water that will quench the thirst of our birth, the thirst for wisdom, the thirst of the soul, the thirst for God's thoughts, and the thirst of hunger, disease, and old age. We must search for this water of the soul, the water of *gnānam* which is the resplendent effulgence of divine wisdom, and the water which flows from the qualities of God.

Where should we look for that water? With wisdom, we must dig within ourselves. We have to dig that well and open the eye of the spring within. We have to open that spring of *gnānam* and continue digging in order to open the spring of our Father. We have to unearth the springs of the wondrous qualities of our Father, *Allāhu ta'ālā Nāyan,* the Solitary One who rules and sustains. They will flow through the ninety-nine nerves. Light will flow within them. Ray after sparkling ray, wonder after wonder will flow through these. We cannot begin to conceive how much will emanate from that spring of *gnānam,* flowing from within wisdom. It is from that spring of *gnānam* that His light, His qualities, His actions, His love, and His grace will flow. That spring will flow through all of the eighteen thousand universes, to us, to everyone. It is only by discovering that spring and drinking its water, the water of *gnānam,* that we can see Him. Those of us who have not attained that state will never be able to quench the thirst of our birth. In this life, we will not be able to understand who we are nor obtain this benefit. We must think about this.

Whether we see the whole world, whether we travel from here to Jerusalem, whether we go to the *Baitul-Muqaddas,*[1] whether we go to Mecca or Medina, whether we travel to the East, the West, the North, or the South, even if we take off from here and orbit in space, or if we come from space and orbit the earth, this does not mean that we have seen or obtained everything. It does not mean we have controlled our minds and seen everything. Did we obtain wisdom? Did we

---

1. *Baitul-Muqqadas*—A name given to the temple in Jerusalem on which site the Dome of the Rock stands today. Literally, the Holy House.

attain peace? Did we find any light? No, we did not. This is what we must search for first.

When we look at the world, it is a history, an example. It is a book filled with examples, with pictures, like the ones hung in every home. The world is a picture. God's creations have been drawn; they are illustrations which can move. We observe those pictures and copy them. But, the pictures that we make do not move. What God creates has life. Each of His creations move, make sounds, and speak. They have taste, fragrance, and innate qualities. There is a difference. They have beauty. They are pictures created by God. As living beings they move about. Some remain in one place, some move around, some go and some come, some live and some die. We can know this. We can understand and realize this. But is it enough to merely see this state? Will we get peace from this? My love you. This will not give us peace.

Precious children, jeweled lights of my eyes, my brothers, my sisters, my daughters, my sons, my granddaughters, my grandsons, my love you. Iowa children, California children, Boston children, Canada children, Connecticut children, all the children of all the Fellowships,[2] all the children who are neighbors, the loving children inside and outside of us, all the children in the East, the West, the North, and the South, all of our brothers and sisters, we give all of you our love. This is the history and the picture that we must understand. When we look at this world, it is all God's art work. Our art work does not speak, but God's art work does. Our art work

---

2. The central branch of the Bawa Muhaiyaddeen Fellowship is located in Philadelphia, Pennsylvania. The Fellowship serves as a meeting house and as a reservoir of people and materials for all who are interested in the teachings of M. R. Bawa Muhaiyaddeen. Branches of the Fellowship exist in the United States, Canada, England, and Sri Lanka.

cannot move. We ourselves have to carry what we make. Who creates things which can move? Can we create them?

God's creations need water, rain, and air. The things we create need nothing. Only some plastic, paper, pieces of dead wood, iron, or clay are needed to create our works of art. Once finished they require nothing more. When making them, we may need to add water and then use air to dry them. We may need to use all five elements. But once we have completed the task, we do not have to nourish or feed them in any way. God, however, constantly nourishes everything that He has created.

This is the world, and all things of the world lie within us. This earth, the world, the sun, the stars, all created beings, everything is within us. Each thought that comes reveals its presence within. As each desire arises, it is projected outside. As each attachment arises, it is projected outside. As each intention dawns, it is revealed on the outside. Every second, they come and go, live and die. We give them form, they appear, and they are soon gone. They keep coming and then disappear. This is our inner state.

What God creates moves, what we create does not. What we create continually destroys us. What we create kills us. Whatever God creates emerges from Him, filled with peace, demonstrating beauty to all, exclaiming, "Look, here I am. This is what your Father created." Each displays its image continually. We must understand this! These beings are also within us. Man is also a creation. He, too, is displayed as an image, as one handful of earth. In this state what must man do? What must he realize? What world is within him? What is inside of him and what is outside of him? Outside is his dream. Inside is his world. He looks at the world known as the mind. He looks at the farm of desire, and he plants the crops of lust, craving, and illusion. He plants the seeds of lust and is so happy, so joyous. Those are the seeds of illusion. He plants them and then laughs, cries, and plays, according to the joy and sorrow they bring. He plants them and tries to be happy. This is the farm where man plants everything, and all that he harvests is *karma,* sin, and evil. The very things he gathers from this farm consume him. They injure him, torment him, and finally kill him. Whether it is a child, a cow, a goat, a dog, or a cat, anything that he raises can kill him. Anything that he raises can torment him. And in the end, he places his hands on his head and cries, or he puts his hands on his cheeks and weeps. Or he covers his nose and cries, or he bows his head on both hands in sorrow. Or he rests his elbows somewhere and puts his head on his hands, or he lies back and laments, "Is this my fate?" Or he looks at the sky and cries, "I am ready now!" or he weeps, lying in a crouched position, and says, "How can I leave this earth?" He cries and cries and realizes nothing. He has nothing.

What is it that must be discovered? When we go to discover the history of the world, we excavate the earth. Certain explanations and proofs are contained therein. So, what must we write about? The book and the wisdom lie within us. Outside are images, which have been depicted as history. "This is Noah, this is Abraham, this is Moses, this is David, this is Jesus, this is Ishmael, this is Isaac, this is Idris, this is Job, and this is Jacob (may the peace of God be upon them all)." This is how it has been represented. "This is a bush, this is a coconut tree, this is a mango tree." They are all there. Having looked at them, we must write about their wisdom *(gnānam),* their qualities, their state, and their taste. From these images we should come to the understanding that the true history lies within us. We have the ink within us. It is the faith, determination, and certitude of *īmān*. With this we must research that history within.

The world is the mind and the mind is the world. The images are there. Desire projects them and then watches them. Some cats catch rats but do not eat them. They eat other things but merely look at the rat. They catch the rat, place it in front of them, and stare at it. Similarly, without any wisdom, we catch the world, place it before us, and stare at it. We keep thinking, "What did I eat before? Should I eat now?" Just like a cat, we catch the world, place it in front of us, and stare. What do some cats do? They watch the rat and as soon as it moves, they bat it around. They bat it a short distance, run, and pounce on it again. Some cats will not eat the rat. They leave it half alive, neither killing it nor eating it. In the same way, we toy with mind and desire. We neither eat them nor leave them alone. This is our work. We hold onto mind and desire and constantly smack them around. Meanwhile, it is we, ourselves, who are dying.

This is the world, the one handful of earth. We must open the *ul-aham,* the inner heart. In Tamil, '*ulaham*' means the physical world that is seen, but '*ul-aham*' means the inner heart. Therefore, we have to open that inner heart and view the secrets within. We must understand those secrets and research into them. When we take each section, perform the research, and understand what is within, then we will know what the world is, what heaven is, what paradise is, what the form of a true human being *(insān)* is, and what the forms of animals such as monkeys, dogs, and cats are like. We will understand, atom by atom, every section within us. We will understand all their sounds. We will know the sound that come from each tree, from wire, from iron, from silver, from gold, and from brass. Have you not heard the sound that emanates from copper? Each metal makes a different sound. We contain all the metals within us. Each makes its own sound. Through those sounds we can understand the melody, the rhythm, the history and the lesson that is revealed, and the song being sung. In this state, we must gain understanding and open the spring within us.

We must perform the seven *tawāfs,* the seven circumambulations.[3] The seven *tawāfs* are made up of the five *kalimahs,* God, and prayer.[4] We must understand the five *kalimahs,* and we must understand prayer. What is prayer, *toluhai?* It is not something that gives us problems, *thollay.*[5] Prayer is God and God is prayer. It is to trust God, to believe in Him, and to accept that there is such a One. We pray because of Him. We pray because of God. The five *kalimahs,* God, and prayer are the seven *tawāfs.*

For a true human being, *insān,* these seven joined together are like a mendicant's large pouch.[6] The innermost heart (*qalb*) is such a pouch. Within this pouch exists the wisdom known as the *qutbiyyat.* That wisdom of the *qutbiyyat* is the most miraculous wisdom. It is divine analytic wisdom which can discriminate and analyze. This is called the *Qutb.* It is one of Allah's names. In the state of knowing everything, Allah's name is *Qutb.* From that state, He created another, Qutb Muhaiyaddeen (ﷺ), a pure light. That pure light came as wisdom. To the wisdom known as Muhaiyaddeen, the

---

3. *tawāfs*—The ritual circumambulations done seven times, counterclockwise around the *Ka'bah.*

4. The translation and transliteration of the five *kalimahs* can be found in the Appendix.

5. Bawa Muhaiyaddeen is punning here on two Tamil words. 'Toluhai' means prayer, while 'thollay' means trouble or difficulty.

6. See Appendix for "The Story of the Qutb's Pouch."

section of *tawāf* has been given. This pouch is within
Muhaiyaddeen, and from within it you can take anything
you want. Place the hand of *īmān,* the hand of wisdom,
within that pouch, and you can take anything that is needed.
You can even ask others, "What do you want?" and you can
give them the things they want. "Do you want some water?"
You can give it. You put your hand in, take what is needed,
and give. Allah, prayer, and the five *kalimahs* form that
pouch. This is *tawāf.* This is the circumambulation that you
must perform. Using the five *kalimahs*, prayer, and God, you
have to circumambulate the heart. The *Ka'bah* is there, un-
touched by satan.

Within the form *(sūrat)* of the *Bismin,*[7] is a dot which is
Allāh-Muhammad. Within that is a tiny *Qur'ān.* Within that
is the *sirr* (secret). Within that are the ninety-nine divine attributes *(wilāyāt).* Within that is the resonance of Allah, containing the explanations of all of everything. Within that
explanation are the fifteen realms and the eighteen thousand
universes. Within that are seventy thousand suns, seventy
thousand moons, and countless stars without limit. Those are
the lights, the prophets, the *qutbs,* the saints, the messengers,
the jinns, the fairies, the angels, the archangels, the heavenly
messengers, and the *gnānis* (beings of divine wisdom). They
are there praising and glorifying Allah, beyond all measure.
They join together and glorify God. That resonance is
present all around you, wherever you look.

God has kept that place for Himself. He has no temple in
the world. He has not built a house of worship anywhere
else. There is no special sign indicating a house or possessions
for God. We have built mosques and churches on the out-

---

7. *Bismin* is the shortened form of *Bismillāhir-Rahmānir-Rahīm*—In the
name of God, Most Merciful, Most Compassionate.

side to pray in, but they are dark. They have no light. We must place lights in these houses of God. Some people light candles and say there is light. Others turn on a switch and say there is light. But, when a fuse blows, the lights go out. When the oil runs out in the lamps, there is no light. When a breeze blows, the candles go out, and all night long, it is dark in the house that we built for God. Every mosque, church, synagogue, or temple is built for the purpose of remembering God, for thinking about God, for intending Him and never forgetting Him. When we are confused, at least we can enter these places, bow down, think of God with wisdom, and ask Him to forgive our sins. We intermingle with Him for a while, tell Him of our mental agitation, and ask Him to soothe our pain. Then we will receive a little peace. By remembering Him, people do attain peace. This is why houses of God are built.

It was in order to make people remember God that the great ones who preceded us constructed these buildings. God told them, "Make the people remember Me in some way. I have no form or shape, but somehow make them remember Me. Remind them of Me. Have them call out to Me. If the people do not do anything else, tell them at least to do this."

[Bawa Muhaiyaddeen now turns to address a clinical psychologist who had just returned from Mecca and Medina.]

Can you look at the earth and extract gold immediately? Can you do this? *Thambi,*[8] can you merely gaze at the earth and find gold? Can we get anything we want from the earth simply by staring at it? No, we cannot. Similarly, when we go to Mecca, can we merely look and take whatever we want? If we just look, will we be given what we

---

8. *Thambi* literally means younger brother in Tamil and is used as an endearing form of address for a male younger than oneself.

want? No, we will not. Does it matter whether we go to Medina or to Mecca? Whether we go to the *'arsh* (the throne of God; the plenitude from which He rules) or the *kursī* (the gnostic eye of light; the seat of God's resplendence), is what we need just lying there, waiting for us to take it? No, *thambi,* we must sift and extract and go within.

Recently, another brother, Kelly, was sitting in Medina and crying, "*Yā Rasūlullāh* ﷺ, you have to give our Bawa Muhaiyaddeen health. It will be difficult for us without him. We must gain peace and tranquility through him. He is a support for us to reach You. Give him life. End his illness."

For three days, he went to the mosque and cried like that. And then on the fourth day a group came. The *Rasūlullāh* ﷺ came. He could be seen. The *Rasūlullāh* ﷺ said, "Come here. Look he (Bawa Muhaiyaddeen) is sitting on top of Mount *'Arafāt,* and there are lots of people standing around him. Look at the way he is sitting, covering his head with a shawl." (Bawa Muhaiyaddeen demonstrates how the shawl was worn and comments: Like this, like a Hindu. The *Rasūlullāh* ﷺ also wears the shawl in this way. And people who go on *hajj* also wear their shawl in this way. Some cover their heads, some don't.)

The *Rasūlullāh* ﷺ said, "Look, he is sitting there and others are standing around him." Kelly saw this. I was talking to the people, comforting them, and guiding them, saying, "Go this way. Come that way."

Many people were there. Are we all in Islam? Many people are Hindus, many are Persian, many are fire-worshipers *(Hanal),* many are Jews, many are Muslims, and many are Christians. There are so many languages, so many names, and so many deities. All of them gather there. They come with one face, as children of Adam ﷺ. Someone needs to speak to them. We must comfort each one who comes and send them on their way. One person will speak one way, another will speak another way, and a third person will speak yet a third way. They need someone like me to whom everything can be said. Each and every person should be given what he needs. Their needs should be taken care of. They should be given peace, given advice about what they have learned and other things. Then, the people should be sent on their way. There must be a person to do that. It was said, "Look at the top of the mountain, he is there."

Whatever is needed must be given to each heart. Why? Each step has to be transcended. Each section must be transcended. Each bridge must be crossed. Only when they have all been crossed can one reach that place. And when you arrive at that place, He will be there. When you reach that place, you have no form. You come as His beauty.

Look over there. See the light bulb? Before the light is turned on, we see only a bulb. But after it is turned on, we no longer see the bulb—we only see light. Can we see the bulb when the lights are on? No, we only see light. Similarly, when wisdom comes, we will not be seen. When the light comes, we will not be seen. Only light will be seen. Then we will not wonder, "What is this? What is that?" Nothing else will be seen, only light. Individual faults will not be seen. It is neither this nor that—it is all light. This is all that can be seen. When wisdom, God's qualities and actions come to us, what will we see? Not the 'I'. The resplendent light that emanates from the qualities of God will be within us, and all who look at us will see only that beauty.

What do we see now? When we look with the eyes of beauty, we see only beauty. When we look with the eyes of darkness, we see only darkness. What do we see with a heart that is filled with doubt? We see only doubt. What do we perceive in the scent of a flower? We perceive only its fragrance. What do we see in the dark of night? We see only darkness. Like this, we see things according to the state of our own hearts. That perception is the proof of the state of our hearts.

Similarly, in our worship of God, in the dedications that we give to God, in the prayers that we perform, and in everything that we love, we will obtain the benefit in proportion to the clarity of our hearts. We profit according to the clarity of our wisdom. We gain peace in proportion to our qualities. We need to understand each thing within us. As long as we do not realize that state, it does not matter to which country or place we travel. The things that we need are not things that can merely be scooped up in different places and brought back. You must endure hardship. You have to undergo a great deal of difficulty, open your heart, and look within.

Sometimes a man will beat a drum and announce that one store is holding an auction, that another is being sold, that in another store something is being sold at a special low price, and so on. So says the man as he beats his drum. We hear these announcements, go to these stores, and buy some things cheaply.

But what we are talking about is not like that. We do not beat drums. We must open ourselves and look within. We must go inside and open what is there. We must forget ourselves, open ourselves, and see what is there. We do not go there to look at other people or speak to them. We have to look and speak to only One Person. That is important. We must look at and speak to that One Person. That Person has a representative. See that representative first; find his house and speak to him. Then speak to the One for whom he is a representative. Open that door first. Then, open the other door. This mouth should be closed and the mouth of wisdom must be opened. The mouth of wisdom should become even more exalted, and we should speak with God's mouth, with the qualities of God. Then we can worship Him.

People claim, "I am this race. You are a different race. I speak one language. You speak another. I am this religion. You are that religion." What is the use of speaking about these things? If we go there, all we can carry is this one handful of earth. That is easy. But, we do not know if they will even let us take that earth with us. The customs officers will say, "Where are you taking that earth?" and hold you back. They will ask, "That is our earth! Why are you taking it?" This is the world. You can, however, take what you really need, because that cannot be seen. You can take the essential things without any problem. Is that not so?

In this way, there are some places where we forget ourselves; we forget our state. Our brother was there and saw certain things. At least you have studied English. You have studied much and understand different things. Some of you understand a little Arabic and are gradually learning more. I do not know anything. I do not know English. I do not know Tamil. I do not know Arabic. I do not know any language. I do not know anything. What can I do? If I don't know anything, who am I going to talk to? God has created me too. He told me to go, speak, and return. "Speak and finish your work," I was told. Therefore, I have to speak.

Thambi, you came to me saying, "I could not find anyone to speak to in Mecca and I was upset for three days. I did not know what to do. I was disheartened. Only when I went to Medina did I see a few things." What is the point of that?

Why have you shut the door like that? You have to open your door and let the people in.

My love you, my *thambi*. If a person who raises cats also raises a dog, when the animals get hungry, they will not keep still. The cat will scratch its owner, saying "Meow, meow." It will scratch, saying, "I'm hungry. Give me food." The dog will come and whine. It, too, will paw the ground and pull on his master's clothes. Although the dog and cat do not know how to talk, they communicate their needs. Similarly, even if you do not know how to talk, if you have wisdom, you can speak with him (the *Rasūl* ﷺ). We must open all the sections we have inside.

Precious children, jeweled lights of my eyes, within you there is a house just for God. That is the *Ka'bah,* that is paradise *(firdaus)*. All the prophets, all the good ones from this world *('ālam)* and the world of souls *(arwāh)* are there within it, praying and glorifying God *(tasbīh)*. Their resonance can be heard at all times. The sounds of their constant *dhikr* (remembrance of God), their *salāms* (greetings of peace), and *salawāt* (salutations), the call to prayer, and their prayers are always heard. That is a place which fire can never consume. It cannot be consumed by the elements of earth, fire, water, and air. Satan cannot touch it. Demons cannot come there. Witchcraft cannot take hold of it. Nothing can go to that place. It is that section which is awakened on the Day of Reckoning *(Qiyāmah)*. The soul and the prophets exist there. Nothing can consume that place. Tomorrow *Allāhu ta'ālā Nāyan* (the Lord God Almighty) will awaken that place. On the Day of Reckoning, as soon as He gazes at it, it will arise as a form *(sūrat)*. All will be destroyed but for that. That is what will be raised on the Day of Reckoning. It is His house. That is what will remain. That is the *Ka'bah*. God has created that place within all of us. That place is within man *(insān)*. That mosque is there, within. That is where you must pray. That is the *Ka'bah* which you must place in front of you. The *Ka'bah* on the outside was built out of stone, but this inner *Ka'bah* has been built out of light by the hands of God, and nothing can consume it. You have to keep this *Ka'bah* inside that place within you. And within that, you must keep Allah and the *Rasūl* (ﷺ), and then pray to Allah, the only One worthy of prayer, with the *Rasūl* (ﷺ) as the *imām* (leader of prayer). Do not worship any other.

This is how we should pray. Each child must open his inner heart and pray. When we pray knowing the correct way to pray and the correct way to recite what must be recited, when we establish that state and pray, then we will not be there. Only the resplendence will be present, and those who stand behind us will see only light. My love you.

Sometimes we hold a cross or other items in our hands and then proclaim, "Miracle, miracle, miracle." But this is not truly a miracle. Our faces are our miracle. Our hearts are our miracle. Then when a demon sees our heart, it will flee. When it sees the light emanating from our faces, it will tremble. As the rays emanate and spread out, the demons will cry, "Aghhh!" and run away. The *'arsh* and the *kursī*[9] are here, along with the radiance of the heart. When the heart is made beautiful and the light of that heart is mirrored as a beautiful luminosity in the face, all the demons will flee. That prayer and worship are within us. Without meditating on this and praying there, we cannot travel elsewhere and

9. *'arsh*—The throne of God; the plenitude from which God rules; the station located on the crown of the head.

kursī—The gnostic eye; the center of the forehead where the light of Allah's resplendence *(Nūr)* was impressed upon Adam (عم).

accumulate things to bring back. We go to such places only to control and correct our mind, to control desire and cultivate wisdom; to end our desires, destroy our pride, get rid of jealousy, cut away separations, foster peace and tranquility; to uplift justice, fairness, and unity, and to live together with God, as His children.

The kingdom of man and the kingdom of the world must be transformed into God's kingdom. We must live here in unity. The very place in which we dwell should be the kingdom of heaven. We can experience paradise here, in this kingdom, by destroying the kingdom of hell and making our life exemplify the kingdom of God. We must cut away separations and live together in unity, as one family. Then the light of God will be seen in our hearts and faces. Through that light we will realize that all our brothers and sisters are one family, and we can attain paradise here in this world. We can understand all the questions and the reckoning we will have to face concerning our life and death. We can know who we are and what our lineage is. We can know that we are the children of God.

We must question ourselves before we are questioned in the grave. We must understand whether we are good or evil and discard the evil. We must understand what is good and act upon it. If at the time we are awakened for questioning, we have already died here without dying and we have found eternal life in that death, then, when we are raised, we will have a seal certifying that we are God's children. We should have God's seal placed upon us while we are still here, so that we can be awakened in this way.

We travel around the world only to realize that we are one family, one people. We travel to understand the explanations and the means by which we can realize that clarity which exists within us. Every meaning, every learning, every state exists, each in its own place, and through these we can obtain great benefits. Many miracles, energies, and powers exist within each thing. These can be researched, and we can benefit from them. We should understand how to attain all of this. We should understand that state. Our minds should not tire because we have not yet reached that state. We should not become disturbed or lose our determination. We should continue to strive. We must be strong. We must always be strong no matter what happens. Truth is always strong. We must have faith that whatever we request will be given when we reach into this pouch using the seven levels of wisdom: feeling, awareness, intellect, judgment, subtle wisdom, divine analytic wisdom, and divine luminous wisdom. If we reach into this pouch using those seven, then we can take peace and tranquility from within it and give that to everyone. That is the great blessing we can obtain. That is *tawāf*. To circumambulate the *Ka'bah* is to go around these seven. We must place the hand of *īmān* into this and ask *Allāhu ta'ālā Nāyan* for help. We must delve into our prayers, into the *kalimah*, into those seven faculties, and from within that give to all. That is *tawāf*.

The black stone is the light of the *kalimah* in the hand of faith and *īmān*. We give *salāms* and then we kiss. We give *salāms* to others and we kiss. We perform the *salāt* (five-times prayer) and afterward place our hands over our eyes in order to give light to the eyes. Our eyes already have light, so why do we touch our hands to our eyes after doing *salāt*? We do it to increase the light there. We say *salāms* and then wipe our faces to make them more resplendent. Then we place our hands on our hearts to create peace.

In this way, for each step, word, and action there is a

meaning. On this path we have to ask for forgiveness (*taubah*). We must ask forgiveness for our faults and do *tawāf*. Then we can take from within and obtain peace. This does not mean that we should just take and distribute just anything from within. What needs to come from this inner place are Allah's qualities and His grace. As soon as we take and embrace these, we will receive peace and all else will leave. With firm faith, each child should try to attain this state. You should strive to achieve this.

Yesterday we spoke to the young children, and asked them, "Wherever you may be, wherever you may journey, what do you need most of all?" 'Ilmi said, "Water. We need water to drink." But there are many kinds of water. Which water are you going to drink? Some kinds of water contain poisons and pollutants. So we gave the explanation about water and what kind was suitable for drinking. All of us need drinking water. It doesn't matter whether it comes from the East, the West, the North, or the South. Can we drink sea water? We have to drink water from a pond, a river, or a well. It does not matter what color the water is. All that matters is that it is drinkable. We gave this explanation because of what 'Ilmi said.

Similarly, it does not matter what race or color we are, what language we speak, or what country we live in. We are all children of Adam (ﷺ). It does not matter how we worship, where we have been, or where we have traveled. What do we need? We need water. We need grace (*rahmat*). What do we need? We need One God. What do we need? We need one prayer, One God. There is only one kind of water which can overcome hell and quench the thirst of our souls. God and His children are one family. To live as one family and worship the One God—this is all we need. This is our drinking water. Whether we are in the East or West, no matter what color we are, whatever language we speak, what do we need? All we need is water to quench our thirst. We need only truth in order to worship God. His qualities are all we need in order to embrace Him. Love is all we need in order to have unity with all lives. We cannot do anything without these things. Other than these, there is nothing else. All else will perish.

Poisonous qualities will kill us. When we travel into the desert, we will perish, one by one, if there is no water. No matter how vast the ocean is, we cannot drink that water. Similarly, no matter how much race or religion we have, we cannot drink that; we will only know thirst. Each one of us will leave the others behind and flee. When an atom bomb is dropped, everyone scatters trying to escape. In a fire, everyone runs, shouting and looking for their own child. Others may refuse to leave, and so they die. Each one looks out for himself. If we get rid of the qualities which seek only our *own* escape and survival and gather the qualities that value the welfare and survival of all, then we can know this peace, this beauty, this light, this state, and this story. This story exists inside of us, in the sky, in the earth, in God, in *awwal* (the time of creation), and in all of the creations of God. We can understand it. This is the explanation. These are some of the histories that we have to understand within ourselves. Through the outer examples, we can gain that understanding within. This is the history that we must understand. We have to reflect upon this. Jeweled lights of my eyes, Professor, Doctor *thambi,* and each child, you and I, we must all understand this. These are the stations that we have to attain.

The destruction of the world is approaching rapidly. The

sun rises and sets quickly. Man is born and swiftly dies. Wealth comes and goes in a flash. The seasons are changing rapidly. Rains and hurricanes are coming quickly. The hues and colors of the flowers are blooming and fading very fast. Everything is fast. Fruits grow and flowers bloom and rot quickly. A time of great speed has come. The rays and lights are changing. This state has begun, and destruction is swiftly rushing toward us.

One country is fighting another country, still another country is waging war. A sister is beaten by her brother, a mother is killed by her son; this is how it will be in times to come. One race destroys another and so on. There will be destruction like this everywhere. Later there will be destruction caused by extremes in climate, by famine, or by racial hatred. The time is approaching when all will be destroyed by storms and gales.

We must escape before this occurs. We must correct and reform our hearts. We must firmly establish the connection between ourselves and God. We must recognize our heritage. We are all from the one family of Adam (☮). We must establish the connection of love, embracing all, gazing at everyone with the same face of light. In order to live in peace and tranquility, we must establish these connections and strengthen our *īmān*. It is only by doing this that we can attain peace. This is the wealth we will attain. This is the treasure we need to gather within ourselves; we must collect the gems and gold within. We must understand and extract the treasures of God, truth, and peace from within ourselves. We must search for wisdom and its capabilities within ourselves. If we have a *shaikh* of wisdom as our guide, then he will be our support in finding all of these within ourselves. May you and I think of this. May God help us.

All the children in Iowa, I give you my greetings, my love. All the California children, the Boston children, all the Canadian children, the children in all the Fellowships, all the Overbrook children, all the Pennsylvania children, all the Fellowship children, all of you, let us all unite and strive as one. Let us become one and work together in order to reach the One God.

There is only one family and One God. He is our heart, our life, and our body. Let us always praise and pray to the Father of our soul. Let us all unite as one and work together. May we be like that. May God help us. *Āmīn. Āmīn.*

As-salāmu 'alaikum wa rahmatullāhi wa barakātuhu. May the peace and blessings of God be upon us. *Anbu.* Love. If there were any mistakes in what I said, please forgive me. If I said anything wrong, please forgive me. May God protect us. *Anbu.*

April 28, 1985

6
A Story of Rābi'ah ﷺ

At one time Rābi'atul-'Adawiyyah 🕮 set out on a pilgrimage to Mecca and the *Ka'bah*. Ibrāhīm ibn Adham 🕮 was also on his way to Mecca.[1] But it took him fourteen years to reach Mecca. Every two steps he would stop to perform the ritual prayers, and whenever he passed a mosque, he would go inside and pray. After fourteen long years, Ibrāhīm 🕮 finally arrived at the mosque in Mecca, but he did not see the *Ka'bah*. He ran about frantically looking for it. "Have I gone blind? Do I not have eyes? The *Ka'bah* is not here. Is what I am seeing just a dream? Is what I am seeing false, O God? I do not see the *Ka'bah* here. I have been walking for fourteen years to get here, and all the way, I have been worshiping You, without forgetting You for even one moment." He ran around wailing in this manner, but there was no reply.

So he asked the people of that place, "Where is the *Ka'bah*? I don't see it here."

Finally someone told him, "The *Ka'bah* has gone to see a particular woman."

"What a wonder this is!" Ibrāhīm 🕮 exclaimed. "Who is this woman? She has committed a great sin, by causing so much trouble for us all. It took me fourteen years to get here,

1. Rābi'atul-'Adawiyyah 🕮 is one of the most famous saints in Islam. She lived in Basrah, Iraq, and her life exemplified divine love (*mahabbah*) and intimacy with God (*uns*). (d. 801)

Ibrāhīm ibn Adham 🕮, a famous Sufi, was born a prince of Balkh, Afghanistan. (d. 783) praying all the way, and the *Ka'bah* has gone to that woman! She has caused so much harm to the world. Who is this woman?"

"Be patient, have *sabūr*," the people told him. "The *Ka'bah* will return in a little while."

But he could not bear to wait. "Tell me who she is!" he demanded. "Where is she? What is her name?"

"Her name is Rābi'atul-'Adawiyyah," they replied. "She can be found somewhere in that direction."

Filled with anger Ibrāhīm (ﷺ) went to find her. Finally, he saw the *Ka'bah* and went inside. There he saw Rābi'atul-'Adawiyyah (ﷺ). "What kind of a woman are you?" he demanded. "You have caused the city so much trouble. You have caused difficulties for God and for all the people. You are causing everyone problems. You are just a woman, and you are causing problems for so many people." He shouted, angrily.

Rābi'atul-'Adawiyyah (ﷺ) listened very patiently and finally replied, "Why are you scolding me? I have not done anything wrong. Why do you scold me like this?"

Ibrāhīm (ﷺ) said, "It is because of you that the *Ka'bah* came here. It has taken me fourteen years to walk to Mecca, and when I finally arrived, the *Ka'bah* was not there! See how much trouble you have caused me and the people of the city."

"Very well, O Ibrāhīm ibn Adham. What you say is quite true," Rābi'ah (ﷺ) replied. "But, I did not set out to see what you came to see. I did not ask to see that which you desired to see. You came to see the *Ka'bah*. I didn't desire to see this stone building. I neither loved it nor cared to see it. I only want to see Allah. I need only Allah. I did not set out to see the stone or anything else. I do not desire such things. I did not set out to see what you came for. The only thing I want is Allah. My sole desire is to see Allah. What happened is Allah's work. What can I do about it? It is not my fault if the stone that you wanted to see came here. That is God's work. It is not my fault. I did not set out to see that *Ka‘bah*. I wanted to see Allah."

While she was speaking, the sound of Allah came, "Rābi‘ah, be careful what you say. Be silent. Watch your words when you speak. When Moses came to speak to Me on Mount Sinai, I sent down only a tiny particle of Myself, and the sound of that tiny particle split Mount Sinai into forty pieces. Mount Sinai used to be forty miles high, not its present height. Now it is very small. During the time of Moses, that mountain near Jerusalem was split into forty pieces, and in that instant Moses fell down dead. I sent merely a tiny particle, a fragment of My light, and yet it shattered that mountain and Moses died. Therefore, abandon the idea of wanting to see Me. You cannot see Me. To see Me, look within yourself and be careful. Be careful, be silent," said Allah. "You must reflect upon this."

Then Rābi‘ah 🅐 continued to address Ibrāhīm 🅐, "I did not come here to see what you came to see. You came to see that stone. Take a look at it and then leave. I wanted to see something else. You traveled fourteen years, praying all the way. O Ibrāhīm ibn Adham, do you realize how many days you have wasted during that time? From where you started, it should have taken only thirty days to journey to Mecca, only one lunar month, the time between the first crescent moon and the new moon, yet it took you fourteen years. The prayer that you performed on your journey was but a show for the world. You have actually been worshiping the world. You performed these prayers every two steps so that people would see you, praise you, and give you titles. Not one of those prayers was directed toward God. Your body has aged fourteen years. Do not waste your time in vain like this. Do not waste your time in vain.

"If you had performed just one *waqt,* one time of prayer, truly in the name of God, then the *Ka'bah* would have come to you. You have not prayed even one *waqt,* truly in the name of God. You claim to have prayed every two steps, but your mind desired the world. Your prayer was an outward show and did not come from within your heart. If you had opened your heart and prayed within to God, in truth, for just one *waqt,* then the *Ka'bah* would have come to you. Your journey should have taken only thirty days from the first crescent moon after the new moon to the following new moon, no more. But now you have aged fourteen years.

"If any of us would truly worship Allah for just one prayer, one *waqt,* then seven hundred million years would seem like one day. If any of us prays one prayer sincerely, directing it only to Allah, then that prayer will give him *hayāt* (life) for seven hundred million years. To you, one month became fourteen years. This is the difference. This is but one meaning. This is sufficient.

"If you had truly prayed one time, one *waqt,* the *Ka'bah* would have come to you. You have wasted fourteen years of your life. Now, return, open your heart, and pray sincerely. Then the *Ka'bah* will come to see you." This is what Rābi'ah (ﷺ) told Ibrāhīm ibn Adham (ﷺ).

We must think about this. We must open our heart. If we truly open our hearts, pray to and worship God for even one *waqt,* just once, with complete sincerity, then whatever we intend will come to us. We must reflect upon this. May God protect all of us. *Āmīn.*

July 26, 1979

7

The Battlefield of the Heart

My brother, you are a leader of prayer *(imām)*, and you, my brother, are a religious scholar *('ālim)*. All the children who are here with us are brothers and sisters to you and to us. We may wish to bring them on the good path, but we can only give them what we have.

My brothers, a bulb will give light only if there is voltage in the battery. Then, when we flick the switch, light appears. Is it not so? Likewise, we must charge the battery within us with Allah's power *(qudrat)*, with His grace *(rahmat)*. Then the current will flow to the various bulbs. If the current is present, it will automatically flow and illuminate the bulbs, but if there is no current, the bulbs will not give light.

Divine knowledge *('ilm)* works in the same way. If we develop within ourselves the qualities of Allah and divine knowledge, then that state will automatically influence others. If we are not in that state, this will not occur. Like a battery without power, our state will be weak, and it will not be able to reach others.

The connection to Allah is like that. We must establish that connection within ourselves with unshakable faith *(īmān)*, with patience *(sabūr)*, with contentment *(shakūr)*, with absolute trust in God *(tawakkul)*, with praise for God alone *(al-hamdu lillāh)*, with His ninety-nine attributes *(wilāyāt)*, and with His gracious qualities. If we do not possess and act with these divine qualities, we cannot establish a connection with others. We would be like a battery without power that cannot give light to the bulbs.

The children that we have taught are in this state today, empty-handed. They have no lamp. They live in dark houses, without light. If we had installed the bulbs and correctly transmitted the current, there would be light in everyone's house. That beauty and light would be in everyone's face and heart. None of the children would be distressed or in a low state. This present state exists because we did not understand and act correctly. The teachings we gave, while we were not in a good state, were like writing on water. Will what is written on water remain? No! Even we cannot read it.

We, ourselves, cannot understand divine knowledge (*'ilm*). We have learned the *Qur'ān,* but we have not understood it. Even though we have studied the *Qur'ān,* we have not comprehended its greatness and its explanations. What is the use in learning the *Qur'ān* and expounding upon it to others, if we have not truly understood its exaltedness? How can we make others appreciate its greatness? If we had understood this divine knowledge (*'ilm*), we would have corrected ourselves. Then when we spread this knowledge, others would look at our example, correct themselves, and come to a good state. Wise people, learned experts (*'ulamā'*), the scholars (*'alīms*), saints (*auliyā'*), prophets (*ambiyā'*), honored ones (*hadrats*), those of absolute faith (*mu'mins*), and true human beings (*insāns*)—all such people should first come to this understanding themselves before teaching others. If we attain this understanding and then teach the children good qualities, that would be very beautiful.

We seem to think that we have completed the fifth duty today. Some people who have the money go on *hajj* five or ten times. Many people have done so. Others perform the five times of prayer and circumambulate at the *Ka'bah* every day. We, on the other hand, must travel long distances to the same *Ka'bah* in order to perform *hajj*. Does this mean that those who live and pray in that place all the time have performed *hajj*? Have the people, who live there and perform their five-times prayer regularly and frequently perform the *hajj,* completed their obligations? Have they attained heaven? Death will come to them, too. There is a Day of Judgment for all. There is a questioning on the Day of Reckoning *(Qiyāmah)*. Allah's judgment awaits us. Does *hajj* mean journeying to that place and returning? No! If we go and return, does it mean that we have completed the five *furūd* (obligatory duties)?

There are five outer and six inner *furūd* in Islam.[1] If you do not understand the six *furūd* but have completed the five *furūd* (outer duties), does it mean that you have completed the *hajj,* the final *fard?* This appears to be our understanding of that which is called *hajj.* There are some people who purchase plaques, displaying the title of *"Hajjiyar"* before they even perform the *hajj.* In Tamil this means, "Who is a *hajji?"*[2] This is not Islam.

It is said that if we journey there, we will attain heaven. Having completed the five *furūd,* does anything remain beyond that? There is nothing beyond that. Some people think that after they have completed these five *furūd,* they can commit adultery, usury, and other evil deeds. Just because the five have been completed, they think that it is all right to practice bad qualities such as falsehood, jealousy, and so on.

---

1. See footnote 1, page 35.

2. This is a pun between the two languages of Arabic and Tamil. *Hajji* (A) is a title for one who has completed the pilgrimage, and *yar* (T) means "who." So *"Hajjiyar"* instead of being a title of honor really means "Who has completed the *hajj?"*

Going and coming like this is not the way to fulfill the precept of *hajj*. You should understand what the state of *hajj* truly is.

Hajj means *maut*, death. When the *Rasūlullāh* ﷺ triumphantly entered Mecca and completed the *hajj*, he spoke of his final state. After completing the *hajj*, in the latter part of his life, his *maut*, his transformation, took place. *Hajj* means that the world inside us has died. When we go on *hajj*, our connections to the world should die. If these connections do not die, it is not *hajj*. Even if we pray thousands of times, for thousands of years, at this same *Ka'bah*, we do not necessarily complete the *hajj*. Where is this *hajj?* The pilgrimage takes place in the heart, and if you are in the correct state, the *Ka'bah* will come in search of you. There is no necessity for you to go in search of the *Ka'bah*. When you clear your heart, it becomes the *'arshul-mu'min* (the throne of one with true faith), and that is the *Ka'bah*.

The word *mihrāb* is written there. What does that word really mean? It means a battlefield.[3] The *mihrāb* is a place where fighting takes place. Should you bring swords there? Should you bring troops? No, it is not a place for that kind of fighting. The word *mihrāb* is written there. The *Rasūlullāh* ﷺ wrote it. What does it truly mean? We don't need to bring guns, swords, knives, arms, and ammunition there. The heart is the battlefield where we must fight. The battle is fought in the innermost heart where there are four hundred trillion, ten thousand spiritual energies *(shaktis)*. In the outer *Ka'bah*, there were only three hundred and sixty

---

3. *mihrāb* (A) Literally, *mihrāb* is the prayer niche in the front of the mosque indicating the direction of Mecca. The third verb form derived from the same root means to wage war. Thus, the *mihrāb* is the point of focus which is the instrument in waging the inner war against that which is other than Allah.

idols, but in our hearts there are countless idols. The heart is a battlefield where we wage war against all those idols. This is the battle that occurs in the place of prayer. We have to complete this war, clear our heart, and find peace within.

Without fighting this battle, there is no purpose in going to the *Ka'bah*. The *Karbalā'* is your heart where all the fighting takes place.[4] That is where you must cut and cut and chase away all evils. The heart is the *Karbalā'*. That is the battlefield, the *mihrāb*. There is no other battle that need take place. The fight is with the disturbances in our hearts. The battle in the heart is against envy, jealousy, and differences. The battlefield is in the heart, the *Ka'bah,* the place of prayer. *Hajj* is to fight this battle, complete it correctly, and achieve peace and tranquility. On that day, we will have truly completed the fifth duty. As long as that battle is not finished, we have not completed this *fard*.

The *hajj* led by the *Rasūl* ﷺ took place after the Battle of Badr and the other wars. It was only after all the wars were over and the ten days of fasting were completed, on the day of *'Āshūrā',* that there was a state of peace.[5] Likewise, we should finish the battle in our heart and realize peace. Only if we finish these battles have we completed the *hajj*. The world within us should die. We say that we must fulfill the *hajj,* but this cannot be done in that outer place.

---

4. When Allah ordered the Angel 'Izrā'īl ﷺ to take a handful of earth, from which Adam ﷺ was to be created, that handful of earth gathered from all four directions was placed in *Karbalā',* the center spot. It is also a city located in Iraq, which throughout the ages has been a battlefield; it is where al-Husain ﷺ, the son of 'Alī ﷺ, fought against his enemies. On a symbolic level, *Karbalā'* signifies the battlefield of the heart (*qalb*).

5. The ten days of fasting are in the first ten days of the month of *Muharram,* the first month of the *Hijrah* year. *'Āshūrā'* is the tenth day. The *sunnah* (recommended) days of fasting are the ninth and tenth day. The other days are *nafl* (voluntary).

Mosques do need to be built. But what are these mosques? There are many orphans, poor unmarried girls, destitutes, and widows, and we should assist them. If we can perform that duty properly, then the *hajj* will come looking for us. The *Ka'bah* will come searching for us. Not only the *Ka'bah*, but all the prophets also will come in search of us, all the prophets from the time of Abraham ☿ when the *Ka'bah* was built until the time of the Prophet Muhammad ☿. Along with the *Ka'bah*, they will come to us with love, bringing the benevolence and grace of Allah.

Who performs *hajj* in this state? What *hajj* are you doing? With the money you spend going on *hajj*, you could help someone who is poor or settle a poor young girl in marriage. Some of your neighbors have no livelihood. Not only must they beg, but many must resort to prostitution. You, being rich, go on *hajj* while your neighbor who is of your own blood is experiencing such difficulties. In *Īmān-Islām*, all are your brothers and sisters, all are of one blood. Yet you go on *hajj* without alleviating the suffering of those who are of your own blood. Whom are you searching for there? Allah says that you should do good here in the place where you are. What are you going to do there?

You have to pay taxes on the money that you carry with you into the mosque and on many other things as well. So why not donate part of that money to help the poor and receive some benefits? With this money, you could kindle a light in the home of every poor person. Isn't that worthy? That is *hajj*. You who are in Islam, who are believers *(mu'mins)*, if you do not do this, what kind of *hajj* do you think you are going to perform? To what degree have you progressed in Islam and *īmān*?

If all of us unite, could we not help those in every home

to become good people? If one man is poor, a neighbor who has the means could help by offering him a job. If ten people join together, they could lift him out of his poverty. Ten more could help still another person. In this way, those in Islam should help their neighbors receive grace and wealth, instead of letting them remain poor. If there is an orphan, we should care for him before we care for our own child. If we do this, someone else will come to care for our child.

If you have these qualities of *Īmān-Islām,* then you will be living in unity. Will darkness come and grab you? Will satan come and attack you? You are the *Sūratur-Rahmān,* you are the *Sūratul-Baqarah,* you are the *Sūratul-Fātihah.* You are the *Āyatul-Kursī,*[6] and that *Kursī* must be given *hayāt* (eternal life). We have not understood or realized this. What are we studying? How can we become true believers? If we don't understand this, then we will belong to one of the seventy-two groups and not the one group.[7] What peace will we receive then?

If you are given tasty food and you stuff yourself up to your nose, you will have a sleepless night. You will awaken and be very restless, tossing and turning until you vomit. All

---

6. These are the names of several chapters and verses from the Holy *Qur'ān.* By mentioning these here, reference is being made to the *sūratul-insān,* the inner form of man. The inner form of man is the *Qur'ān* and is linked together by twenty-eight letters. The sounds in the *Qur'ān* which resonate through wisdom, the Messenger of Allah, Prophet Muhammad ⊕, the angels, and heavenly beings all are made to exist in this body as secrets. The *kursī* is the gnostic eye; the center of the forehead where the light of Allah's resplendence *(Nūr)* was impressed upon Adam ⊕.

7. Bawa Muhaiyaddeen ⊕ frequently refers to the seventy-three groups of man. Only the seventy-third group consists of true human beings with perfect faith. Of the other seventy-two groups, seventy have no faith in God and the remaining two have faith, but they also still have a desire for the world and its pleasures. (From *Islam and World Peace: Explanations of a Sufi,* page 57.)

this will happen because you were fascinated by the aroma and taste of the food and stuffed yourself up to your nose. If you had drunk just a glass of water saying, *"Al-hamdu lillāh! All praise is to God!"* then you would have been able to sleep very peacefully with trust in Him *(tawakkul)*. What benefit did you receive from eating so much? A long night of suffering. If you had shared the food with ten others, you would have been happy and the others would have been happy as well. Is that not so? We must reflect on this.

We should reflect on our every action. In Islam there should be no paupers in the congregation. The rich and the poor should stand in a row, as equals, and we must treat all with this same equality in other places as well. In both the mosque and the *Ka'bah,* the king and beggar should stand as equals, and in life, too, we must make the poor our equals. That is Islam. If we make them our equals in this world, then we are true believers *(mu'mins).* That is Islam. But, instead, in the world you discard someone as less worthy, and then when you are in Allah's place of worship, you proclaim all as equal. There is no unity in this. God will be watching. He will say, "You have trampled him in the world, but you come here and act as though he is your equal. You discarded him and caused him great suffering. Now, you come and say that he and you are equal."

Later you will cry, "O Allah, protect me!"

Allah is watching and He will ask, "How can you say that the both of you are equal?" We must think about this. Every child should reflect. All the learned ones *('ulamā'),* the scholars *('alīms),* the honored ones *(hadrats),* the caretakers of the mosques *(lebbes),* the ones who give the call to prayer *(mu'adhdhins),* the wise people, those people who have divine knowledge *('ilm),* the teachers of wisdom *(shaikhs),* the descendents of Prophet Muhammad ⌾ *(sayyids),* all of us, whoever we may be, we should understand and treat all lives as our own, giving them peace and showing them the way. We should have that quality of giving peace.

Reflect. In *Īmān-Islām,* you should provide a dowry and help a poor girl to get married. At weddings in the past, they used to tie a small black-beaded necklace on the bride. Aren't they telling you to use gold necklaces now? The money spent on a single gold marriage necklace could be used to enable so many others to get married with black-beaded necklaces. The black beads have no monetary value. When we wash the corpse, we recite the *kalimah,*[8] and cut off this necklace and lay it by the side. The true value is not in the black beads. The real value is in the love for Allah in the heart.

Take for example the gold jewelry that you wear. If you sold that jewelry, you could help give so many poor girls in marriage. You give a hundred thousand *rupees* as dowry to your own children, yet you do not donate even a hundred *rupees* to give a poor girl away in marriage. You have forgotten the *Qur'ān* and the words of Allah and the *Rasūlullāh* ⌾. One whose heart is dominated by satan is attracted by the wealth that you offer as a dowry, just as a dog is always attracted to rice with a bone rather than plain rice. A dog will never choose the plain rice. Rich people are offering a bone to the dogs, and meanwhile the poor young girls have no food to eat. Those girls lose their *īmān* and certitude and destroy themselves by becoming slaves. I have seen this with my own eyes. So many have gone astray because of poverty. Yet, we all say we are in Islam. What good is this? How can

8. The affirmation of faith—*Lā ilāha ill-Allāh, Muhammadur-Rasūlullāh.* There is no god but God, and Muhammad is the Messenger of God. See Appendix.

those who do not care for their own neighbors and do not help others be in Islam?

I am just talking. Do what you like, but people with wisdom and *īmān* should reflect on what I have said. If there is water in a well, then you can draw that water. Like that, if there is something good in the *qalb,* then that is what will come out. It is according to each one's earnings. We will do our duties, and you should do your duty. All the children should attempt to reach a good state. That will be good. *Al-hamdu lillāh.* All praise is to God.

November 3, 1982

8
Adorn the Inner Ka'bah

Bismillāhir-Rahmānir-Rahīm. (In the name of God, the Most Merciful and Most Compassionate.) The One who created me, O *Rahmān* (the Merciful One), the One who sustains me, the One who protects me, may You protect my children, my brethren, and all those born with me. You formed me, my brothers and sisters, my mother and father, and all of us from one fistful of earth. Other than You, each thing was formed from one fistful of earth, the size of its own hand, and this must be returned to the earth in the end. Each thing, even the ant, grows to eight-spans of its own hand. The creations eat from the earth and grow on earth. Finally in the grave, they have to return one thousand fistfuls of earth. This is what man gathers from all that You have cultivated on this earth.

The water and blood that are joined and connected to this one fistful of earth are related to the human race. Other creations, such as cows, goats, birds, and fish also emerge from this same earth. Thus, they have a blood connection to man and are also created as food for mankind. On one hand, they strengthen the body of man, and on the other, they have this link, this unity with the form of man. This is how mankind is manifested and nourished.

Man has a similar connection to the earth and the ether. One is above and one is below.[1] What is in between are the

---

1. This concept is discussed in depth in *Sheikh and Disciple* by M. R. Bawa Muhaiyaddeen ☙, pages 3-4.

scenes of his mind and the dramas that he enacts. Between the two is the school where man understands the section of creation. This is what is called a *Ka'bah*.[2] It can be a place of worship, a place of heaven, or a place of hell. It can be God's kingdom or the kingdom of hell. According to the way each person constructs this place, he will experience joy or suffering. This is part of what he must learn for his final exam. He can assume a form belonging to a particular race, religion, or caste, or to animals and demons. He can take a form that kills and eats another man. Man assumes a form *(surat)* and then nourishes that form. But, that very same form will later devour him. A person can only live as a true human being if he reflects upon this with the wisdom of man and with God's qualities, intentions, and thoughts. Anyone who does not reflect in this way will find it very difficult. He does not realize what his end will be.

The One who gives us the undiminishing, limitless wealth of grace and incomparable love, the Ruler of the universes *(Rabbil-'ālamīn),* the Most Merciful, Most Compassionate *(ar-Rahmān, ar-Rahīm),* the Sustainer, the One of grace, the Beneficent One—that One alone understands everything. We are all one society, one race, one religion, one group. We may speak many different languages, but as babies, we speak all the languages in the world, the language of the birds, the language of the East, West, North, and South. The moment a baby is born it makes a sound, "Ahh, ooh, amma." It is the same sound in any language. A baby knows all languages and all religions. But as we teach them, we graft our own learning onto them. We teach them to say "ABCD" or to speak Arabic, or something else. We graft things onto them

---

2. See page 51, "Whatever a man considers as the focal point in his life is his *Ka'bah.*"

and say, "We belong to this group, we belong to that group." As the child gathers these, its earlier connection with God is cut away. The unity of mankind that it knew earlier is severed. The unity of love that it had earlier is cut away. The 'I' and blood attachments develop, and the differences of "You are my relation!" emerge. These things arise within him and cause him to commit sins and even murder. *Karma* emerges and strengthens all these qualities.

Precious jeweled lights of my eyes, Allah gave countless words of wisdom *(ahādīth)* to the *Rasūl* ﷺ. He sent down 6,666 verses *(āyāt)* of the *Qur'ān,* relating all the accounts about the earlier prophets. He displayed the unity that all are of one father and mother. "I am the Primal Father of all. I am beyond the beginning and end. I am the One who created all of you. I am the One who gave you all these things to rule over. I gave you food, a body, and a soul. Your perceptions and your intentions are the connection between you and Me, between the children and the Father. It is the connection between this world and the kingdom of God *(arwāh).* I have done all this to teach you what I have learned about how these connections arose." *Allāhu ta'ālā* (God Almighty) said this.

"Realize this. Understand this. You are not worthless beings. When you realize this and understand, there will be no difference between you and Me. You will be within Me and I will be within you. You can speak from within Me and I can speak from within you. What you need you can ask from within Me and what I need I can ask from within you. The entire kingdom is within you and within Me. The world *('ālam),* the divine kingdom *(arwāh),* and all of everything are within us. Understand this, O man. Divisions do not exist, not one or two or three, not any. Everything is within us."

Allah said this, revealing the exaltedness of human beings and of their qualities and actions. You must understand this.

He said, "*Yā Rasūl*, I have not formed this *Qur'ān* separately. In the divine kingdom *(arwāh)*, in the beginningless beginning *(anāthi)* before the beginning *(āthi)*, when I manifested you, I formed every letter of the *Qur'ān* as light, as life *(hayāt)*, each one scintillating. The letters are glittering and shining with this life. I spread these throughout the light of *Nūr Muhammad.*[3] This is the light I placed on the forehead of Adam and all the other prophets. I asked all the angels *(malaks)* and archangels *(malā'ikat)*, 'Who will accept this light?' No one would accept it. All the other lights were swallowed by this light.

"Then the earth came forward and said, 'I will accept this light.' Because the earth came forward to accept it, I had to establish unity between the elements. Earth, fire, water, air, and ether were enemies to one another. With the light of *Nūr Muhammad,* I united these five, and the arrogance of each one was controlled. They were united and made to accept the one *kalimah.*[4] That *kalimah* contains so much compassion and mercy. We made them recite that *kalimah* and acquire patience *(sabūr)*. With these five, I created the form of man with clarity. This clarity is the exaltedness of man *(insān)*. Nothing could grow without this life, in the world *('ālam)*, in the divine kingdom *(arwāh)*, or anywhere. Every drop of water, every leaf, every fruit, nothing could exist without this

---

3. The beauty of the qualities and actions of the *wilāyāt* (powers) of Allah; the radiance of Allah's essence, or *dhāt,* which shines within the resplendence of His truth. It was the light of Muhammad ☺ called *Nūr Muhammad* that was impressed upon the forehead of Adam ☺. Of the nine aspects of Muhammad ☺, *Nūr Muhammad* is that aspect which is wisdom.

4. The affirmation of faith. *Lā ilāha ill-Allāh, Muhammadur-Rasūlullāh.* There is no god but God, and Muhammad is the Messenger of God.

life. Each has that light of grace. Each has an atom of light from that resplendence. Cells, viruses, nothing could grow without that atom of light. Whether it be water or fire, things that move or things that do not move, such as stones, everything grows because of this life within it.

"The *Qur'ān* is the history of all this, and I have kept it within the form of *insān*. I have kept everything within him. I have kept it within the *Nūr* and spread it everywhere. All of everything is within the form of *insān*. That form is not a simple one. The eighteen thousand universes, the world (*'ālam*), the divine kingdom (*arwāh*), and all of everything exist within him. The grace and wealth of God are within him, the blessings of God are within him, the triple flame[5] is within him, and the wealth of the three worlds is within him. One has the potential to become either a human being, an animal, or a satan.

"Whoever understands this state, this body, will know that the *Ka'bah* is his heart. His body is the form of the world, the *sūratud-dunyā*. When he looks at this world, when he looks within at this *Sūratul-Fātihah*,[6] he will see that his heart is the *Ka'bah*. This heart is the throne of a true believer (*'arshul-mu'min*). He will see this heart of grace. That is heaven, the place of worship, and all the stars are made to shine within him."[7]

Allah said to the *Rasūl* ﷺ, "*Yā* Muhammad, for one who understands this while in the world, I will adorn his *Ka'bah*,

---

5. Allah, the *Nūr*, and the *Qutb* ☼.

6. See footnote 5, page 38.

7. The stars refer to the twenty-eight letters of the Arabic alphabet. Each section of the human form is represented by one of these letters. When man purifies himself, these letters take the form of light and appear as the *Ummul-Qur'ān*, or the eternal source of the *Qur'ān*, which was revealed to Muhammad ﷺ.

his heart, like a bridegroom. I will decorate the entire place and gather together all who loved, worshiped, and prayed to Me. I will make them appear as beautiful maidens, who will enchant all the universes with their light and beauty. I will bring all of them from this world *(dunyā)* to the divine kingdom *(ākhirah)*. I will bring them to paradise *(firdaus)*."

The *Ka'bah* is not what you see on the outside. All these letters are within this body. The 6,666 verses *(āyāt)*, and so many words of wisdom *(ahādīth)* are within this form *(sūrat)*. In one fistful of earth, there are so many atoms of light. They are there in every grain of sand. All these lights are in the world of the body, the *sūratud-dunyā*. Within the sheath of the *kalimah*, God will adorn man's entire body with light. The form of such a one becomes illumined, his qualities are transformed into maidens, and his heart is ornamented with all the beauty, qualities, actions, and conduct of Allah that he has acquired. All these are like celestial maidens. All the prophets and the others who prayed in this heart are gathered together as one. All are there within the heart—the angels *(malaks)*, the archangels *(malā'ikat)*, those with divine wisdom *(qutbs)*, the saints *(auliyā')*, and the prophets, such as Adam, Noah, Abraham, Ishmael, Moses, David, Jesus, Muhammad *Mustafar-Rasūl (Sallallāhu 'alaihi wa sallam)*, Job, Jacob, Idris, Isaac, Joseph, Solomon, Salihu (may the peace of God be upon them all), and all the others. Having thus been adorned, all of God's family are raised up together.

This is how the heart will be decorated. This body that is the world should also be decorated like this. We should give up the world that we are carrying. This is what we must accomplish with our prayers. Every word must make our body resplend. Every word must be made into light. We must make every thought and every intention resplend. We must make every gaze resplend within Allah's gaze. We need to transform our qualities and actions into Allah's and make them resplend. With true faith and certitude, we must transform our body into the form of light and make it beautiful. This form must shine. Some people say, "Look, that body is shining. You can see the light!" They can see it. So many thousands of people have said this to me. They can see this body resplending with light. Inside, everything is beautifully decorated. That is heaven.

God has kept an outer *Ka'bah* as an example, saying that this is what the prophets built. Inside, as well, the prophets, the *qutbs,* the lights of God *(olis)* gathered one fistful of earth to build this. All joined together to build this. Although it is not an easy task, we, too, must prepare this place. We must make this place beautiful. We must decorate this place inside and be able to see it. Allah, the prophets, the *qutbs*, the saints, the lights of God, and many others are there. We are not separate from them, and we are not different from one another. "I am one race, you are another race. I am one color, you are another. I am from one family, you are from another." None of these differences exist there. Allah, the prophets, the *qutbs,* the saints, mankind, all the children of Adam ﴾ﷺ﴿ are one family. Anyone who sees two is in hell, while anyone who sees unity and one race is in heaven. One who sees divisions is in hell, and one who sees unity is in Allah's kingdom.

There are six lives that resplend as one. There are the seven states of consciousness—feeling, awareness, intellect, judgment, subtle wisdom, divine analytic wisdom, and divine luminous wisdom. The sixth state (divine analytic wisdom) is the wisdom of the *qutbiyyat*. Divine luminous wisdom (the seventh state) resplends as Allah's wisdom, as the *Nūr*. The six lives function as this one life, as Allah's life, as the *Nūr*, the seventh life. It resplends as wisdom, light, completeness, and as Allah's qualities. The qualities that resplend with this beneficence are Allah's qualities. The kingdom that is prepared with these qualities is Allah's heaven. Through this form and these actions, one must prepare this heaven, Allah's heart, His secret, and His essence *(dhāt)*. The world of His essence is within the heart. The world of wisdom exists within our heart as light. The prophets, messengers, and *qutbs* dwell there. That is the world of light, the world of *hayāt* (eternal life). The soul exists as the *Nūr*. The realm of the *Nūr* is Allah, the grace of all the universes *(rahmatul-'ālamīn)*. We have this vision of plenitude within us.

During our life *(hayāt)*, we gather heaven, hell, joy, and sorrow. We pray, we worship and go to churches, synagogues, or temples in order to understand what we have gathered. We have gathered these things, believing in them. But when we look within, we see that some of these things have taken the form of satan. They exhibit such signs. Some have taken the form of the angels. There are signs indicating that, too. Some have been formed out of fire and have taken the form of jinns. They have those signs. Some have assumed earth forms and we pray to them. Within the body, there are millions of forms such as snakes, scorpions, and centipedes that we worship.

The resplendent beauty of Allah, that star, that light has no form, no shape, no figure. When you fashion the form of *insān* (a human being) and look within, Allah will be within that form. When man makes all the letters resplend within and focuses intently upon them, he becomes an *insān*. He resplends with the resonance of *Nūr Muhammad*. When you look at that resplendence, it will be a mirror. You will see the universe *('ālam)*, the divine kingdom *(arwāh)*, and all of everything shining within it. When you look at that resplendence, that light will be Allah. When you gaze into this mirror, you will see yourself. You will have become young. The beauty you see will be your own beauty, and within that, you will see Allah's beauty. Man will see Allah's beauty within his beauty, and Allah will see man's beauty within His beauty. We must adorn ourselves in this way.

As long as this does not develop within us, as long as we do not attain this state, as long as we do not know this prayer, this path, as long as we do not know this *dhikr* (remembrance of God) and these qualities, we remain separate from the truth. From whom are we separate? We are separate from God. To whom are we enemies? We are enemies to truth and unity. What have we done? We have changed from a human being into a beast, from *insān* into *hayawān*. Without knowing the correct way, we have changed our beauty and our form to a lower state. We must think about this.

Precious children, this is the *Ka'bah.* The throne of pure faith *('arshul-mu'min)* is the heaven to which we must go. This is where Allah speaks within us, where *insān* exists within Him and speaks to Him. When man understands the earth and discards it, he becomes the original *insān,* the form of light. And when he sheds even the light form, he becomes complete. What is that completeness? It is Allah. While in the form, we must realize what needs to be discarded and what should be kept. Without cutting and eating a fruit, how will we know its taste? Similarly, we must cut every quality, extract the juice, taste it, and discard what is not needed. We must cut our learning, our wisdom, our studies, our words, and our actions, chew them, squeeze them with wisdom, and see. Until we do this, we will suffer.

You must reflect upon this. God created all these wonders for you to reflect upon and understand. He made them beautiful, adorned them, and kept them all in the form of love. In the state of unity, we are in the form of the *Qur'ān.* We are in the form of light and letters. That form will shine. It will glitter. There will be lightning. All kinds of things will happen. What we see depends upon when and where we look. *Al-hamdu lillāh,* all praise is to God! We must think about this.

My brothers and sisters, daughters and sons, grandsons and granddaughters, we must prepare ourselves to come to this state, to praise the Lord of all the universes *(Yā Rabbal-'ālamīn).* We must come forward to prepare ourselves. We must strengthen our faith, certitude, and determination *(īmān).* If you hurt your own heart, whom does it hurt? It hurts you. You think you are hurting others. But no, you are causing pain to your own self. When a lizard sheds and drops its spines, we may get pricked if we are not careful. We experience the pain, not the lizard. Similarly, along the road satan drops all kinds of illusion *(māyā)* in our path. When that pricks us, the pain is ours, not his. All the suffering comes to us. Therefore, whatever comes, we must correct ourselves, have tolerance and forbearance, and cut away what needs to be discarded. That will be good. Reflect. Try to unite and live as one heart. Melt as one heart and taste the honey that flows from that one heart. Taste that and see. *Āmīn.*

This is all for today. All praise is to Allah. May the peace of God and His beneficence be upon all of you. *(As-salāmu 'alaikum wa rahmatullāhi wa barakātuhu kulluhu.)*

March 23, 1985

9
The House of Prayer

Those who are born with me, as the life within my life, gems who are the lights of my eyes, children who are the wisdom within my wisdom and the love within my heart, I give you my love.

My precious jeweled lights, my children, this world is like an egg. So much good and bad can hatch from within it. So many things take form and emerge from within it. Many elemental energies (*shaktis*) and creations appear. Energies that are good, bad, dark, and light all form to become an embryo, and emerge from this egg of the world.

If you first look at this egg, it appears to be just a dot, but when you examine it more carefully, you see that it is a world. When you look even more intently, you find that it is a world of illusion, and when you examine that, you find a world of magic. As you look still further, you find a world of arts and drama, and as you continue to look, you see a world of torpor. When you look carefully at that, you see a world of intoxication and lust, and when you gaze carefully at that, you see a world of darkness. As you look still further, you find it is a world of hell, containing poison and millions upon millions of venomous beings. When you examine that world of hell, you find that its depth is limitless, endless, and that it is impossible to lift anyone out of its fire. This is the world of sin.

All these join to form this egg of the world, and everything that hatches from it lies within that circle *(sukūn)* as an embryo. Everything in the world hatches from that embryo and exists within this body. Everything in this world, both seen and unseen, is within this body, within this one fistful of earth, this embryo which is a dot. Everything is within the circle of the *mīm* (م).[1] When you gaze intently at this circle, you will see that it is tied within the *wāw* (و).[2] If you look at that carefully, it will be seen as *sunīyam*, or black magic.[3] Adam and Eve (☮) were bound within this *sunīyam*. To separate ourselves from that and emerge is prayer or worship. Only after we free ourselves from this *sunīyam* will we enter the state of realizing true prayer.

The world might say many things about prayer, but true prayer is purity. Prayer is purity. Every group has a particular method of prayer, worship, meditation, and devotion. These have been given many names. We must reflect upon the states of prayer that exist today. True prayer is purity. There are many things like this that we should know and understand.

Islam proclaims that today is the end of *hajj,* that today is the final day of the fifth *fard* (obligatory duty). This is the day one dies. Whoever is born must die one day. One has to die in order to worship or pray. That is *hajj.* According to the teaching, today is the day to complete the fifth *fard* of *hajj.*

The prayer of *hajj* cannot be done at home. A person must

---

1. *Mīm* is the Arabic letter (م) which corresponds to the English consonant 'm'. In the transformed man of wisdom, *mīm* represents Muhammad (☮). The shape of the *mīm* is like a sperm cell, and from this comes the *sukūn* or circle, which is the form of the world.

2. The verb used here for "to tie" is *kaddu* (T) which means to bind by spells and magic. *Wāw* is the Arabic letter corresponding to the English consonant 'w'. In the human form made of the twenty-eight Arabic letters, the *'wāw'* denotes the genital area.

3. *sunīyam:* Black magic; sorcery; enchantment; ceremonial defilement; illusory vacuum; chasm.

travel. Whether to a jungle or a desert, he must journey somewhere and then pray there in order to fulfill this *fard*. When a person dies, what do you do with the corpse? You take it to a cemetery. Like that, one must die to fulfill this fifth *fard*. Until now, he was entangled in the world, in desires, wife, house, and property. On this day, he gives what needs to be given to the world and dies to everything in the world. This is the journey he must take in order to fulfill this *fard*.

From this day on, the world within him dies, desire dies, the mind dies, and the connection to the body dies. All the blood ties, bondages, and attachments within him die. His house, his country, and his titles die. According to the true meaning, today he should wear the shroud of a corpse. Whatever his destination may be, he has to journey in that shroud and then pray. Those near Mecca might go to Mecca and pray. Those in a different country might go to a jungle and pray. Those who are in the countryside might go to pray by a lake or near a tree. Wealthy people might go to a mosque and pray. Like that, people can pray in various ways. The one who has nothing might pray by the roadside. Today is such a day.

The *Rasūl* ﷺ was given the revelation *(wahy)* that this fifth *fard* of *hajj* should be done in Mecca. But, the point is not that you have to go to Mecca to complete this prayer or that you must go to Medina to complete this prayer. What is really meant is that man must go beyond whatever world lies within him. He has to leave behind his desires for gold, wealth, and women. All these desires should die. He should wear the shroud and go. When he goes in this state, he will have no relatives, no attachments or bondages. He will be a pauper. On that day he is a corpse. He goes in that form and gives all responsibility to God.

Of the five *furūd* (obligatory duties), this is said to be the final *fard,* where one dies. After one completes this, he does not return to the world to marry, work, or gather property. He dies in this prayer. This is how such prayer is performed. When he performs the *hajj,* he must give away everything he possesses and die. All that he has accumulated within his heart, be it his wife or child, house, properties, or wealth, must all die within him. He must give full responsibility to God, and Allah must be his only treasure. Allah alone must be in his bank. Allah alone must be there in his innermost heart *(qalb).* Only Allah must be in his prayer. Only Allah must be in his worship. Only Allah must be in his thoughts. In his love and in his longing, only Allah must be present. In everything, only the treasure of Allah must be within him.

Hajj is to reach the state where you possess nothing but that wealth which is Allah. Allah is the only wealth for one who has fulfilled this pilgrimage. That is the wealth for his birth, his death, his prayer, and his hunger. That is his only wealth at all times. To reach this state is *hajj.* If anyone can complete this state of *hajj,* then he is truly a wealthy man. He will be wealthy in all three worlds: the beginning, this world, and the hereafter *(awwal, dunyā,* and *ākhirah).* He will be a representative and a judge for these three worlds. When he reaches that state, he will be a light to the three kingdoms of God. He will be a judge and a trustee to these three kingdoms.

One who has not received this wealth has not yet died. He has wasted his time. Allah has given this prayer as the fifth duty. If you look closely, no one in the world actually does this. No one. Is there anyone now who has done this? During his time Muhammad, the *Rasūl* ☧, performed this *hajj.*

Since then I have not seen anyone who has completed this.

Some lazy people go on *hajj,* just to escape from their families, their wives and children whom they are unable to support. They are so lazy that they go and eat what others provide. They call themselves renunciates *(sannyāsis),* holy men *(swamiars),* or saints *(auliyā'),* but they are, in truth, just lazy people! There are many people like that. But do you think such a one has died to the world? In reality, he has simply joined the society of lazy people.

Both the *Rasūl* 🕊 and 'Umar ibnul-Khattāb 🕊 fulfilled this *hajj.* In the past, there were some saints like Uwais al-Qarnī 🕊 and Rābi'atul-'Adawiyyah 🕊 who also accomplished this, and there may have been others as well.[4] But, in today's world, we have not seen anyone who has truly performed the *hajj.* About one thousand, three hundred years ago such people did exist, but today we cannot say that anyone has fulfilled the fifth *fard* in this way. Nowadays, the *hajj* is like a tourist's trip. Everyone goes and howls and shouts there, so we also shout. All go to pray, so we also pray. Everyone goes on *hajj,* so we also go. Everyone eats, so we also eat. All bathe, so we also bathe. All are slowly dying, so we are also dying. This is what we are doing. We are not doing anything different.

It is only after you die to all five that you can pray to God and reach Him. Only after that will you have the strength of *īmān* and the wealth of Allah. True prayer is known only after the five duties are completed.

---

4. 'Umar ibnul-Khattāb 🕊—One of the most steadfast companions of the Prophet 🕊 and also his father-in-law. He later became the second caliph of Islam.

Uwais al-Qarnī 🕊—A mystic from Yemen and a contemporary of the Prophet 🕊.

Rābi'atul-'Adawiyyah 🕊—See footnote 1, page 83.

Now my precious children, what is prayer? Prayer is purity. Does that mean you need to build a mosque or church? Is that prayer? See how many churches there are. Each church might cost a million dollars. How many millions of dollars have been spent building these? Today, if you look, what do you find within the churches? You find bats, birds, geckos, and spiders. Some churches lack sufficient funds, so there is no light inside. There are millions of churches and schools like that.

When there is no income for a religion, there is no place to pray to God. To establish a religion requires income. You need money to pray to God, because you need money to build churches. Later, if the income diminishes, they close. Then what? Can you truly pray to God in these churches and mosques? Is it only when you attend such places that you can pray to God? Is this our rightful prayer? No! Anyone praying to God should understand that prayer is purity. It is an individual matter, where each individual prays for himself. Prayer is the state in which there is a connection between man and God. Prayer must be perfectly clear, without any blemish. This is prayer.

How can we perform this prayer? To whom shall we pray? In order to pray to God, one must construct the place of worship within oneself. One has to build that temple, mosque, or church by oneself, inside oneself. One has to build that place of worship within and make it pure. One must provide light for that mosque and make it one's own. At every moment, with great care, one must tend it, keep it clear, and see that there is always light inside. This will be one's own place of prayer, one's own mosque, the place where one can worship.

Until one does this for himself, until one prepares that

mosque within, until one has built that place of worship, all one's prayers, devotions, and meditations will never be right. It will be like a house of worship that has been closed for lack of income and is now full of bats. If you go to a place where religions congregate, what will happen? Someday, when arrogance comes, there will be separations, and it will close. Places like this are not true houses of worship. The house of worship one builds within is the correct one. Each one has to build his own platform for prayer, his own place of worship. He must build his own palace, spread his own prayer mat, and pray alone, for himself. This is pure worship. Until one builds such a church for oneself, one continues to reside in the world. But once one builds a church within, then one is in the kingdom of God, the correct place of worship.

Prayer means to fashion this church within. Prayer is to build a temple of God in your heart. You must construct this place with the qualities, behavior, and conduct of God, with the justice and actions of God. You must keep it pure. In that church, you can pray whenever you intend, whenever you wish. It will always be open for worship. Once it is built, you must be the one who does duty in that church. When you serve there, each and every breath, every moment, will be a prayer. You will not see any sin there. You will see nothing other than God there, and you will not speak anything other than the speech of God. Why? Because you are performing duty in His temple. You are worshiping Him and seeing only Him. In that state, there is no other speech.

Precious children, gems of my eyes, this is what true worship is. Castes, sects, and religions all appear to be high and exalted, but these differences are the lowest of evils. If you look outwardly, they appear to be exalted, no doubt. Why? Because, they are in the majority. They have more votes.

They may be larger in number, but it does not mean that there are more people truly worshiping in those places. Each proclaims to be of a higher caste or a superior religion, but having such differences is the lowest of evils. For exalted beings of divine wisdom *(gnānam)* who see everything as equal, such differences do not exist. All these things do not exist for one of divine wisdom.

What difference does that Eternal Primal Treasure show? What difference does He show? He has no differences and His devotees have no differences. Anyone who is a slave to God has no racial differences, no caste differences, no status differences, none of these. Truth is a point, prayer is a point, and the world is a point. God resides where truth and prayer unite as one. Hell lies where darkness, torpor, and the world join together. Let us understand this today. It is through the fifth *fard* of *hajj* that we can truly understand this.

Today is the day one leaves behind his present state, dies, goes to God, and surrenders to Him. Today is the day one gives everything away that he has accumulated in this world and surrenders to God. One becomes an orphan without anyone and says, "O God, but for You, I have no other support. There is no other god for me, no other helper, no other resource, no wife. There is nothing for me but You. I have nothing else but You, O God. Please accept me." On this day, we offer this supplication, surrender to Him, and accept only Him. Today is the day we surrender everything and accept Him, saying, "We have no country, no house, no child, no wife, no attachments, no wealth, nothing. We have nothing, O God. Except for You, we have nothing." Today, we go and surrender to Him in that state. Today is the day we honor God. Today, we give all responsibility to God and accept Him. That is the fifth *fard*. Having done this, we realize what prayer and meditation truly are. Having done this, we find the way to reach Him. There are many, many opportunities like this.

This is the day that we call the day of *hajj*. This is the day of the fifth *fard,* when we journey forth and pray to God. What is this prayer? What is this journey? It is the day we leave our cage, our mind, our desire, our qualities, and go beyond. It is for this state that the name *hajj* is given. But, instead, we go by plane, land there, and shout, *"Kajj, mujj!"*[5] and then return. Once a husband and wife went, shouted like that, and returned. They were swindled out of half of the money they brought, and with the rest, they bought goods and returned home, declaring that they had performed *hajj.* Only if one goes and does not return is it true *hajj.* The one who left is gone. When that one does not return, that is *hajj.* All those who go and return have not truly performed the *hajj.*

There is much to say about this *hajj.* My precious children, today we must try to understand what it is that we truly need. Therefore, my precious children, build your own place of worship. Build that church in your own heart. That church will always be yours. No one else can lay claim to it. Each one's church is one's own. Build your mosques individually. That is your house. No other heaven will be given to you. The mosque that you build yourself is your heaven. Your place of worship is your heaven. The house that you construct is yours. If you build a house in the kingdom of God, that house becomes yours. If you construct your place of worship, that is an exalted place. That is the kingdom of God, the house of God for you. He will give you the house

---

5. A meaningless jumble of words.

that you build. He will give you that which you praised. He will give that wealth to you. You must understand this.

You must make that place of purity perfectly pure and perform pure worship in a state of purity. If you build that church of purity with purity, it will become your own. Please, my jeweled lights, establish this state. As long as we do not build this church and establish this state, we are like Canada geese. When there is wind and ice in one place, the geese migrate elsewhere. They may even go as far as Sri Lanka. When the seasons change, they return. Half may die and half return. Our worship is like the migration of these geese. For a certain time we do this, and for a certain period we don't. Some geese die from the ice, the cold, the gales, and the winds and some return. Some die and some come back. In the next season more die. This is how it is. This is the manner in which we attend our places of worship. We go according to the season, like Canada geese. That is not prayer. We must build the house of worship within ourselves. Let us prepare that place of meditation and prayer and reach a state of purity.

When we stand in front of a mirror and look at our face, we can see anything that is amiss. There might be dirt on our faces from working in the kitchen or performing some other task. When we look in the mirror, we immediately clean ourselves. A place of worship is God's mirror. With every breath, we must observe our face in His mirror. Whatever work we do, when we look into that mirror, we will notice any dirt, and immediately we must clear it.

God is a mirror of light. When we dwell with Him, we must wash the faults that come with every breath. When we are with Him, we can see every thought and intention and the dirt and darkness on our faces. Anger, sin, arrogance,

he black stone is the light of the kalimah in the hand of faith and īmān.

—M. R. BAWA MUHAIYADDEEN

envy, deceit, desire, lust, or something else may arise within us, but the moment one of these appears, we will observe it in that mirror. Then we must wash it off immediately. This is what we must do.

Once we build that place of God, it becomes a mirror. Our form will be beautiful once we go to that place, look into the mirror of God, and clean every thought, everything that comes to our mind, at each and every moment. Our hearts and faces will be beautiful. If our hearts (*aham*) are clear, then our faces (*muham*) will be clear. If our prayer is clear, our church is clear. If we are clear, then God is clear, and everything can be seen.

Therefore, my precious jeweled lights, in our hearts we must establish faith, certitude, and determination, strengthen *īmān,* and try to build a place of worship. Each one has to build his own house of worship, his church. You should be ready to pray at any moment. You should be ready to perform this duty each and every second, without ever forgetting. Precious jeweled lights, until we do this, our life is like that of the Canada geese. It is like the clouds that move with the gales, disperse, and come together again.

My precious jeweled lights, we must try to build our pure place of worship. We must take this journey of *hajj.* Let us understand this *hajj.* There are five and six causes in man.[6] We see the five elements outside and six spheres or worlds inside. Outside, we see earth, fire, water, air, and ether. They exist as the body. Those are the five outer duties. Within, we see six other causes. We see the lights within our eyes. We must reflect on that. We perceive a fragrance within our nose. Ponder that. We hear the sound within our ears. Reflect on that. We perceive the taste in the mouth. Reflect on

---

6. See footnote 1, page 35.

that. We see a light within our heart. Reflect on that. These are the things we see inside. The ears, nose, eyes, tongue, the inner heart, and wisdom—these are six instruments. We must analyze these and understand. Then the beauty will be in the face. We must realize these six beauties within. These are the five and six causes. When five and six are added, it makes eleven. The number eleven looks like two legs. One with two legs can either be a man or a monkey. One can be man-God or man-monkey. We must understand this.

If man truly understands the elemental energies (*shaktis*) of the five outside and the six within, he would understand God. If a man truly understands these eleven, he would understand the eleven zodiac signs and would pray to the twelfth, which is God. The eleven planets change but that final planet never changes. God never changes. These are the twelve openings: the two eyes, two ears, two nostrils, one mouth, two openings below, the navel, the *'arsh* (the crown of the head), and the *kursī* (the third eye in the center of the forehead). These are the twelve openings, the twelve planets. They are the ten sins, the *Nūr* (the resplendence of God), and Allah, the *kursī* and the *'arsh*. These twelve are in man. When we properly reflect upon these twelve, close the ten and open only the two, that is *hajj*. Prayer is performed only after this occurs. The *'arsh* and the *kursī* must be opened. Then you can see God. That state of worship is purity. The ten must be closed. All the pleasures of these ten must be removed. Let us gradually remove them. They can be removed little by little.

You must build this church. With faith, certitude, and determination, you must try to search for that wealth which is God. That wealth will never change or diminish. It will be useful to you in any country, whether it be here or elsewhere. Money taken from one country must be exchanged into the currency of the country you are visiting. But, no bank is needed to change that wealth which is God. It will be accepted everywhere; it has value everywhere. That is the wealth of grace. Such wealth is of tremendous value everywhere and never needs to be changed. That is an unchanging wealth in any country. Your worldly wealth, your money, and even the language you speak change according to the country you are in, but God's wealth is unchanging, for the entire universe, for all of everything. Wherever you go, it is valuable. That is the wealth of God.

Let us try to attain and keep in our hearts that one treasure which is God. If we can possess that, we will have obtained that limitless wealth, that perfect and complete wealth. We will be the princes of God. We will be the vice-regents of God. We will be the owners of all three worlds, and we will realize that we are the rightful owners.

My precious children, let us reflect upon this, build a place of worship, and understand where it is that we must worship. It is good to understand this prayer and act accordingly. Let us try. That is purity. My love to you all. My greetings to you.

November 11, 1978

10
May Our Intentions Be Fulfilled

Bismillāhir-Rahmānir-Rahīm. (In the name of God, Most Merciful, Most Compassionate.) *Yā Allāh, Yā Rahmān* (O God, O Merciful One), may You protect, nourish, and sustain us. *Āmīn.*

Yā Allāh, who is limitless grace and incomparable love, the One who gives us the undiminishing wealth of grace, You alone are the One with such plenitude and with the perfection of these qualities. There is nothing, no one in all the universes who has the plenitude and qualities that You have. You have no form, You have no color. Indeed, we have not seen You. You have no father or mother. You were not born. You are not ruled by hunger, disease, old age, and death. There is no house that You call Your own. We have never seen Your kith or kin, wife or relatives. It is impossible for us to find You, to discover You, through relatives, by Your address or Your house.

You are the *Ārumattavan.* You are the One who has no one to call Your own, yet we cannot call You an orphan or a pauper. You are the *Ārumattavan,* the One who is devoid of the six evil qualities of lust, anger, miserliness, attachments, bigotry, and envy. You are the One who is devoid of the five elements—earth, fire, water, air, and ether. You are the One who does not have a created soul. All other beings are given life through the soul which will be called back in the end. You are not like that. Such creations appear and disappear, but not You. We can see You through Your qualities, Your actions, Your trust, and Your faith—through these and by no other means. We need to discover You by discovering the words within Your words and by finding the actions within Your actions. We must conduct ourselves within Your conduct and thereby come to understand Your conduct. We must look from within Your vision, and only when we have Your vision will we see You. When Your sound comes, we must go within that sound and discover Your sound. When Your speech comes, we must go within it and discover You. It is in this way that we can realize You. Other than this, there is no other means to find You.

The four hundred trillion, ten thousand 'spiritual' forces, the jinns and fairies, ghosts and demons, dogs and cats, monkeys and birds were all created by You, yet each one proclaims, "I am god." They each perform their own supernatural feats *(siddhis)*. Even the snake, holding its poison within, displays its power. It spreads its hood and hisses, exclaiming, "I will kill you." The bull has two horns and warns, "If you come close, I will gore you." The lion roars, baring its strong teeth. It displays its strength and proclaims, "I will kill you and eat you." Every creature, each creation of Yours, uses its own qualities to display its own miracle. Through its qualities, actions, and strength, it proclaims, "I am great."

Similarly, four hundred trillion, ten thousand people separate themselves through varied beliefs and worship these 'spiritual' forces as gods. Because You cannot be seen, people make things and beings that they can see into gods. They make gods out of the things they can reach out for and touch. Even though fire can burn them, some people worship that very same fire. If a poisonous snake bites a man, he will die; yet man worships the very snake that can cause his death.

In this way, man worships things capable of destroying

him. The things that he worships cannot create and cannot protect him from death or destiny, yet each proclaims, "I can do it." But, in the end, having danced their dance of arrogance and displayed their strongest energies, they will say, "It is impossible for me to help you. This is your fate or destiny as ordained by God." It is like this in the world.

In the beginning, God created the children of Adam ⊛, mankind, in an exalted manner. From time to time, God sent the various prophets, but still these qualities, these visions, and these gods filled every man's heart and body. In this state, no one worshiped God. Man made rocks, rain, earth, fruits, animals, birds, snakes, monkeys, donkeys, and horses into gods and worshiped them. However, there were some with wisdom who declared that there is an all-pervasive power called God, an almighty power common to all, indivisible, without any form, either manifest or hidden, an omnipresent power. That power is One. In the world, there have been men of wisdom who did say this, but still, the people did not seek God, find Him, and worship Him. It was during such times that God sent the prophets. Each one brought different aspects of the teachings. Finally, the *Rasūl* ⊛ was sent. In all, God sent 124,000 prophets, beings with divine analytic wisdom *(qutbs)*, and saints *(auliyā')*. Of those, twenty-five prophets who had great clarity are mentioned in the *Qur'ān*.

The precepts of the five and six *furūd* have been explained through the *Rasūl* ⊛. Of these, the five *furūd* (obligatory duties) are the easy ones. First, believe in Allah, have full faith in Him. Second, worship Him alone, saying there is no God other than Him. Third is charity, or *sadaqah*. Whatever we have, even if it is only one handful of food, we must share in unity. We are one family. Hunger is one. Our speech, our minds, and our lives are all one. We must live as one family, not as separate individuals. We must experience life as one, be it in hunger, death, or eternal life *(hayāt)*. We are all children of one mother. Such unity is Islam. It is for this that we have the *kalimah: Ash-hadu al-lā ilāha ill-Allāhu wahdahu lā sharīka lah, wa ash-hadu anna Muhammadan 'abduhu wa rasūluh* (I testify that there is no god but God; He is One without associates to Him, and I testify that Muhammad is His servant and His Messenger). Through this *kalimah,* we must accept the *Rasūl* ☬, accept Allah as the One God, and become one family. We must try to attain this state and become one family. This is the meaning of that *kalimah.* Attaining this state is Islam. We must transform the qualities we have kept within us and reclaim those which we discarded. We have kept race, religion, color, animals, and snakes within us, and we have driven away God and His truths. We must chase these things away and bring God and His truths within us.

Sadaqah is charity. At some point, we may even have to offer our body, our very life. We must always be prepared to share whatever pertains to the body. This is charity. But, if we do not observe this *fard* (obligatory duty), then we have the fourth *fard* of fasting. We must try to realize ourselves through fasting, to see how we feel when hungry. See how weak, dazed, and faint we become when we fast. This happens when we fast for just one day, between the meal *(suhūr)* eaten before the early morning prayer *(subh)* and the sunset prayer *(maghrib)*. We are fasting for just one day between early morning and sunset, from dawn to dusk. Within this short time, how fatigued and tired we feel! We must remember those who are starving, day and night, having no food whatsoever for long periods of time. We must at least know and experience the plight of those brothers and sisters who may be starving because of poverty and resolve to share our food.

Out of the twelve months of the year, *Ramadān,* the month of fasting, is but one month. During this month, we must realize the many qualities grouped within us. We are giving blood and nourishing these groups which belong to satan. We are nurturing these groups that belong to ghosts and demons, to the base desires *(nafs ammārah),* to the attachments and cravings belonging to hell. We nurture this hell, this world. Within, we nurture so many germs, so many thoughts, ghosts, and demons, all of which are enemies to God. We give them our blood, making them grow.

My true brothers and sisters, Allah created you out of earth. Every creation was made from earth, fire, water, air, and ether. Allah formed each and every creation from the five elements. Every creation, every form, is made from these five. Reflect upon this! This is why Allah decreed the duty of fasting. But, even after fasting, we do not realize the brotherhood of man, and that is why the fifth precept of the *hajj,* of holy pilgrimage, was prescribed.

This is now the month of *hajj.* The *Rasūl* ﷺ brought the *kalimah* and unity. He brought forth what Allah told him and gave it to the people. But, they attacked the Prophet ﷺ with all the forces they had. They attacked and chased him away, utilizing the energies they had within themselves. They were told not to drink alcohol, not to steal, not to eat food which is forbidden *(harām),* and not to cheat others. In this way, the Prophet ﷺ exhorted the people to rid themselves of these evil qualities of satan. They were told that they must not strive for selfish gain, that they must not live just for themselves, and that they must treat everyone with equality. Prior to this, people cheated, told lies, stole one another's food, stole the property of others, and ate prohibited food. Because the people enjoyed all this freedom, they opposed these new laws. It was to change these practices that the *hajj* was made obligatory.

The Prophet ﷺ said that we must follow these five decrees and progress, little by little. He said that we must perform the *hajj* and come to realize the three thousand gracious qualities of God, His ninety-nine powers *(wilāyāt)*, His qualities, His actions, and His conduct. Through those qualities and conduct, we must merge with the plenitude within. This is the way to finally perform that pilgrimage called *hajj*.

Because the people were unable to accept the advice of the Prophet ﷺ, the fighting began. They attacked him with all the evil qualities they had within themselves, with hypocrisy, vengeance, and deceit. They attacked the *Rasūl* ﷺ. They attacked God, the *Rasūl* ﷺ, truth, *īmān,* faith, and trust. They attacked all those who were good and who spoke the truth. They retaliated against the tongue that spoke the truth. Mothers were separated from their children; children were taken from their mothers; brothers and sisters were divided; families were shattered and scattered in all four directions. Their houses and property were destroyed. They were chased from their homes, flushed out of hiding and attacked. They were pursued and hunted down. Even while fleeing in fear, they were murdered. This is why the battle of Badr and many other battles came to be fought.

The *kalimah* was given to drive away these evil forces and bring about peace and unity, allowing brothers and sisters, mothers and fathers to unite as one. It was given so that prayer to God, truth, and *īmān* could unite in the face of all these evil forces. A few did achieve this state of faith and trust. They followed the words of the *Rasūl* ﷺ, the words of Allah, and little by little, their unity grew. By following the Prophet ﷺ, they accepted and followed the truth with perfect faith. They had firm faith that there is no one worthy of worship other than *Allāhu ta'ālā,* God Almighty. They worshiped only Allah and nothing else. They prayed without holding anything as equal or comparable to Him. They understood the difference between bad and good *(sharr* and *khair).* They accepted this and avoided what was prohibited in their food. Evil and good are in Allah's responsibility. Knowing what was permissible and forbidden *(halāl* and *harām),* they conducted themselves, discriminating between right and wrong, good and bad. Afterwards, they understood the nature of charity *(sadaqah).* They understood the meaning of prayer and charity. But even those who accepted the *kalimah* were not free from their base desires. Because they had not escaped their *nafs,* they still had to undergo many difficulties.

The *Rasūl* ﷺ took what each person had and was prepared to give, and then he distributed it amongst the poor. The Prophet ﷺ counseled the people to give to the poor while keeping some money for basic expenses. Like this, he continued explaining the precepts up to the duty of fasting. But even though the Prophet ﷺ did all this, the people did not allow him to remain in Mecca. He and his followers were chased from their city, from their dwellings, all the way to Medina. The Prophet ﷺ reached Medina with seventy followers. Once they established themselves in Medina, so many wonders occurred. Mothers, brothers, and sisters accepted *īmān* and joined in unity. The *hajj* was the time that they all came together as one. The wars had ended, the evil people had been destroyed, enmity was gone, and peace prevailed. On the day of the *hajj,* the hearts of the people softened, and fathers, mothers, and children united in peace. They understood the place they were born, the place where they dwelled, the place to which the prophets came, what happened earlier, and what was yet to happen. They traveled to those places and to the places where the Prophet's companions had died. They did what was needed and found peace. They remembered the faithful ones who died and remembered their actions. That was the day of the *hajj*.

Hajj is to reflect upon all those who have died and all that has transpired, to clear and open our hearts, discarding all our failings and differences, and to unite as one on the straight path. We unite and say, "We are believers *(mu'mins)*. This is Islam," and we conduct ourselves with faith on that path, following behind the *Rasūl* ﷺ. In this way, once a year, we Muslims, wherever we may be, those of us who have *īmān*, gather together in one place. This is *hajj*, the fifth *fard* (obligatory duty). But it is not merely a gathering. The true meaning is to conduct ourselves accordingly. Merely performing the fifth *fard* of *hajj* once in our lifetime is not the true requirement.

We come together in Mecca and Medina on the outside, but Mecca and Medina exist within us as well. Just as we perform *hajj* on the outside, inside, we must recognize good and bad, right and wrong, heaven and hell, Mecca and Medina, the human being and Allah. All these exist within. All the evil qualities within us, the base desires *(nafs ammārah)*, the ghosts and demons, the satans, the bad qualities of haughtiness, vanity, and pride; arrogance, *karma*, *māyā* (illusion); *tārahan*, *singhan*, and *sūran* (the three sexual energies which are the sons of illusion); desire, anger, miserliness, infatuation, fanaticism, and envy; intoxicants, lust, theft, murder, and falsehood; jealousy, treachery, vengeance, deceit, sorcery, incantations and tricks *(mantras* and *tantras),* magic, mesmerism, witchcraft, and all such qualities, along with the thoughts that belong to satan, have seized control of the Mecca and Medina within us. We have to eliminate all of these qualities. Just as we establish unity outside, we must realize unity within ourselves. Every child must fulfill that *hajj* within.

The angels, the archangels, the prophets, the enlightened ones, those with divine analytic wisdom *(qutbs),* the saints *(auliyā'),* and all those living in this world who have pure faith *(mu'mins)* come together on the outside on this day of *hajj.* In the same way, they must also gather in unity within our heart, along with the three thousand gracious attributes of God. That is where we must build Mecca and Medina.

How do we do this? Whatever the *Rasūlullāh* ﷺ said and did there, we must do the very same within our hearts. We must prepare ourselves by acquiring within our hearts the same actions and qualities as the *Rasūlullāh* ﷺ had. We must construct this house inside our hearts. We must build a place of prayer to Allah within our hearts. Before our death, we must die in that place where we pray to Allah. We must die within Allah. It is there that we find heaven *(swarnam* and *swarakam).*

In that outer place, we meet with the true believers *(mu'mins)* once a year. All with *īmān* gather there with love. We meet them with love and joy. Just as we would meet them on the outside, we must also give life to that intention, focus, and unity inside our hearts. Within, we must have the thought of all joining together, working as one, praying and living together in unity, forever. Whether it be in joy or in sorrow, we must have the intention and focus to exercise the qualities of patience, contentment, trust in God, and praise for

138 HAJJ: THE INNER PILGRIMAGE

God (sabūr, shakūr, tawakkul, and al-hamdu lillāh) and say,
"God is great! Allāhu Akbar!" This is what we must strive
for.

Whether we have something in abundance or nothing at
all, we must say, "Allāhu Akbar. God is great. Bismillāhir-
Rahmānir-Rahīm. In the name of God, Most Merciful, Most
Compassionate." If we have nothing in our hands, we should
reflect, "What do other creations do?" A chicken doesn't
carry any food. It scrapes the earth with its feet and finds
food. A bird pecks at leaves, flowers, or fruits and finds food.
A bee sits on a flower and extracts honey. Others find their
own nuts and fruits. They do not store vast quantities of
food. Each one uses either its intellect or wisdom to find food
whenever it is needed. We, too, must use our analytic wisdom in this way. God has given us seven levels of wisdom.
He has given us hands and legs. He has given us a wide open
space. We must search for and find our food. It is not necessary to steal, to murder, to tell lies, to cheat, or to attack someone and take his food for ourselves. We have eyes, ears, a
nose, and a mouth. We can do the work of a laborer, or cultivate a farm, or cut wood to sell. We should be able to do
something to earn an honest living. In this way, we can earn
enough to feed our stomachs. If we find a neighbor in need,
we must be able to feed him, appease his hunger, and bring
him along the right path.

We must realize and learn within ourselves what true fasting really means. We must know the true meaning of the hajj
within ourselves. In Īmān-Islām there are the five and six
furūd. The fifth and last fard is hajj. When we go on the pilgrimage once and come back, we have finished all five. Then
what is there to do after that? This is not all there is to hajj.
This outer pilgrimage is just to exemplify the state we must

attain within. We must take these principles and discover the meaning within. It is only when we complete the *hajj* within ourselves that the true *hajj* has been fulfilled. At that time the world *(dunyā)* will die within us, and we will be free from this world, having reached a place which is good *(khair)*. Evil *(sharr)* has ended, and we have died and disappeared in goodness *(khair)*. We have disappeared in the path of Allah. We suffered in evil and have now disappeared into goodness. We must find life *(hayāt)* through death *(maut)* and find a place where we can disappear within Allah, within His wealth *(daulat)*.

When the sun sets, the light disappears. The colors and the rays disappear. The moon also sets and disappears. In the same way, when we leave this earth, we must leave all the suffering of this world and disappear. That is *hajj*. When we leave behind our qualities and establish a connection with Allah, adopt His qualities, perform His actions, disappear within Him, and merge with Him, only then will we fulfill the *hajj*. It is on that day we have completed the *hajj*.

On the other hand, look at those people who have been born in Mecca and Medina. They perform the *hajj* every year. It is said in the *kalimah* that to truly fulfill the *hajj* with *īmān,* at least once, is important. There are some people who are wealthy enough, but they are unable to go on this pilgrimage to Mecca. It is said that if they help the poor, giving charity and whatever is needed, that will fulfill the *hajj*. We must understand what *hajj* truly means. Suppose we go all the way from here to Mecca and Medina, walk around, eat, ask our petitions *(du'ā')* of God, and return. That does not mean we have completed the *hajj*. We come back with what we brought with us. We come back with the base desires *(nafs ammārah)* and the monkeys that we took with us.

So what *hajj* have we performed? For a short time, while we are performing the *hajj,* we are in that correct state, but when we finish and return, we still have all that we took with us. When we make all the qualities that are inside us die, before we return, that is *hajj*. When we annihilate all these qualities and replace them with Allah's qualities, that is death *(maut)* and eternal life *(hayāt)*.

It is impossible to complete all that can be said about the *hajj*. We have spoken about it so many times in so many different ways. *Al-hamdu lillāh*. All praise is to Allah. *Allāhu Akbar!* Allah is great. Almighty God, may You fulfill all our intentions. We must try as hard as we can. We must perform our duties. We must understand the truth and try to attain the goodness that results from that. We must strive to do this. *Al-hamdu lillāh*. All praise is to God.

August 26, 1985

Appendix

Al-Kalimatul-Khams
THE FIVE KALIMAHS

AL-KALIMATUL-ŪLĀ
THE FIRST KALIMAH

Lā ilāha ill-Allāh, Muhammadur-Rasūlullāh.

There is no god but God, and Muhammad is the Messenger of God.

AL-KALIMATUTH-THĀNIYAH
(ash-shahādah)
THE SECOND KALIMAH
(The Testimony of Faith)

Ash-hadu al-lā ilāha ill-Allāhu wahdahu lā sharīka lah;
wa ash-hadu anna Muhammadan 'abduhu wa rasūluh.

I testify that there is no god but God. He is One without associates to Him; and I testify that Muhammad is His servant and His Messenger.

AL-KALIMATUTH-THĀLITHAH
THE THIRD KALIMAH

Subhānallāhi wal-hamdu lillāhi wa lā ilāha ill-Allāhu
wallāhu akbar. Wa lā haula wa lā quwwata illā billāhi
wa huwal-'aliyyul-'azīm.

Glory is God's, and all praise is God's, and there is no god but God, and God is most great! And there is no majesty or power except in God, and He is exalted, supremely magnificent!

143

AL-KALIMATUR-RĀBIʿAH
THE FOURTH KALIMAH

Lā ilāha ill-Allāhu wahdahu lā sharīka lah;
lahul-mulku wa lahul-hamd; yuhyī wa yumīt;
biyadihil-khair; wa huwa ʿalā kulli shay'in qadīr.

There is no god but God, He is One without associates to Him. His is the dominion and His is the praise; He bestows life and death, in His hand are the blessings, and He is omnipotent over all things.

AL-KALIMATUL-KHĀMISAH
THE FIFTH KALIMAH

Allāhumma, innī aʿūdhu bika min an ushrika bika shay'aw-
wa ana aʿlam, wa astaghfiruka limā lā aʿlam, innaka anta
ʿālimul-ghaibi wash-shahādah. Tubtu ʿanhu wa tabarra'tu ʿan
kulli dīnin siwā dīnil-Islām, wa aslamtu laka wa aqūlu:
lā ilāha ill-Allāh, Muhammadur-Rasūlullāh.

Dearest Allah! I seek protection in Thee against ascribing any partner to Thee knowingly, and I beg Thy forgiveness for that which I might do unknowingly—indeed, Thou art the Knower of both what is seen and what is hidden. I have turned from such faults and I absolve myself from every sort of creed except pure belief in and surrender to Thee, and I commit myself wholly to Thee saying, There is no god but God, and Muhammad is the Messenger of God!

Labbaik

*L*abbaik: "Here I am." The opening words of the *Talbiyah,* the most frequently used prayer for *hajj* and *'umrah* (the lesser pilgrimage). When Abraham ⌣ was directed by Allah to build the *Ka'bah,* he was also told to call the people to the house of Allah to worship Him alone. The *Talbiyah* is an answer, an acknowledgment to this call.

After donning the garb of *ihrām* and making his declaration of intent, the pilgrim immediately begins reciting the *Talbiyah.* The recitation of the *Talbiyah* is returned to again and again throughout the pilgrimage:

> *Labbaik Allāhumma labbaik.*
> *Labbaik lā sharīka laka labbaik.*
> *Innal-hamda wan-ni'mata laka wal-mulk.*
> *Lā sharīka lak.*

Here I am O Allah! Here I am!
Here I am, there is no one who is Your partner, here I am!
Surely, all praise and blessings are Yours, and dominion.
There is no one who is Your partner.

The Story of the Qutb's Pouch

The Qutb (Muhaiyaddeen 'Abdul-Qadir al-Jīlānī ☺)[1] journeyed on a boat to an island, where he came upon a king's orchard. The orchard was huge, filled with guavas and so many other fruits. The Qutb ☺ was very young at the time, only fifteen years old. When he saw the fruits, he crept into the orchard and picked and ate just one.

A guard caught him and struck him, yelling, "You thieving little boy, you little thief. You dare to come into the king's orchard and eat his fruit!" One hand was by his side, and with the other he hit the Qutb ☺ on the cheek.

The Qutb ☺ was slightly angered by this, but said, "What I did was wrong."

The guard ordered, "I must take you to the king."

"I did not know this was the king's orchard," the Qutb ☺ explained.

But still the guard held him and said, "Come." He went to strike him again, but his hand became like a piece of dead wood, and he could not hit him.

"O God, you have made me receive a blow from the hand of an unbeliever," the Qutb ☺ said, "O God, forgive me. You have made me subject to this state."

Then the sound of God came, "Look, you will see that it was written in *awwal,* at the time of creation, that you must

---

1. The saint of Baghdad was born in Naif in the District of Jīlānī in Persia on the first day of the month of Ramadān in the year 1077 A.D. He died in 1166 A.D. See Glossary: *Muhaiyaddeen, Qutb.*

receive a blow from his hand. Through you, this guard will be brought onto the good path. The only way he can be turned to the good path is for you to receive a blow from him. Look it is written there!" God said this to him.

"O Qutb, first and foremost, you must have *sabūr* (patience). Until you finish this work, have *sabūr*. Do not become so upset over these things. Do not become angry when such things happen."

Heeding these words, the Qutb ⏄ tried to appease the guard, "Let me go now, and I will give you seven fruits in place of this one. I only picked one, but I will give you seven in return."

"You thieving boy," the guard shouted. "Where are you going to get seven fruits when you had to steal this one?"

"No, these seven are truly mine, and I'll give them to you," the Qutb ⏄ insisted. He reached into the pouch at his side, pulled out seven guava fruits, and gave them to the guard.

"Hey, where did you steal these from?" the guard challenged. "Where did you get these?"

"They are truly mine. They came from my garden." Then the Qutb ⏄ had him look into the pouch. There within the pouch were the seven oceans, the seven worlds, hell and heaven, all of creation, the king, the entire world, the guard's house, everything. Everything was within that pouch.

The guard was astonished. "Is everything in there? Are you a god? Of what nation are you a god? *Aiyō,* O great one, I hit you! O please forgive me. Where do you come from?"

Then the Qutb ⏄ opened his mouth and told him to look into it. The eighteen thousand universes and everything in all of existence could be seen in his mouth. It could all be seen in the bag and in the Qutb's mouth. All the worlds, all creations, the sky, the earth, the sun, the moon, everything could be seen there.

"Oh what a sin I have committed!" the guard cried, and he ran to tell his wife. *"Aiyō,* I do not know what land this god has come from, but I struck him. And then I saw such wonders in the pouch by his side. I saw you and me and all the worlds in that bag. He opened his mouth, and when I looked into it, I saw such incredible wonders there. The heavens, the *'arsh,* the *kursī,* the pen of God, the kingdom of God, the throne of God, everything was there. I could see everything."

"You are such a sinner," the wife scolded. "He is a god! With which hand did you hit him?" When he showed her, she took a knife and cut it off. "Now, we must go to him," she said, and they took the hand with them.

The Qutb � was sitting in a certain place, in accordance with the word of God. They fell at his feet, and the wife pleaded, "O holy one, I have punished him for the fault he committed. Please forgive my husband! O our god, please forgive us. O light of God, O holy one, please look upon us and take us on your path."

"It is all right. Give me the hand." The Qutb ⌐ placed the hand back on the guard's arm, stroked it, and it joined together. Then he taught them the *kalimah* and told them, "Be happy now."

∞

It is like this. All the universes and everything in existence are within your mouth. Your truth, your words, your speech, your actions, your intentions, your prayers, your worship, divine knowledge—all these pearls are within your mouth. These gems are all within your mouth. The eighteen thousand universes, heaven, and hell are in your words. Wealth and poverty are in your words. The pearls and the gems that come from your tongue, the eighteen thousand universes, and heaven are all within you. In the same way, your life is in that pouch by your side. What you do, the goodness you seek, all your good and evil, everything is there in that pouch. Everything you spend, everything you have done, everything you give, everything you have received, your prayers, your worship, your intentions and actions are all there in your pouch. Your profit and loss are there. Depending on how you lead your life and conduct your affairs, it is all there within that pouch of your heart. It is all there.

If you open that heart, within it you will see the gardens, the orchards, the kingdom of God, the kingdom of justice, the kingdom of peace, the kingdom of tranquility, the kingdom of the freedom of life, unity, and the kingdom of harmony in which all lives are your life. If you can open your heart and look at your intentions, your focus, your unity, your exalted qualities, your outspread duty, and your wisdom; if you can perform your duty working together as one life; if you can open your heart and see all that has been cultivated there, then there is nothing that cannot be found there. You will be able to give and receive anything; you will be able to realize any level of bliss. It is all there in that state.

This is the treasure that we have to find within ourselves. Those qualities and treasures are there. If we open our mouths, such beauty is there, such happiness, such wealth. Divine knowledge, or *'ilm,* is the pearls, diamonds, gems, and jewels. If we open the heart, all of the worlds and eighteen thousand universes will be there. There will be no life that does not dwell there, no being that is not in existence there.

You and I are within each heart. If you attain that state and open your heart, then everyone can be seen in that mirror. If the *'ilm* that oozes from God's qualities, His wisdom and His actions come from that mouth, then when you open that mouth what pours forth will be the bliss of the eighteen thousand universes and heaven. Peace will be there, and each life will be comforted by your loving touch. If you are in that state, each word will embrace and stroke the hearts of others. We must fashion this within us. If you are in that state, that is the Qutb (ﷺ).

October 9, 1983

Glossary

The following traditional supplications in Arabic calligraphy are used throughout the text:

ﷺ following the Prophet Muhammad or *Rasūlullāh* stands for *sallallāhu 'alaihi wa sallam,* may the blessings and peace of Allah be upon him.

ؑ following the name of a prophet or an angel stands for *'alaihis-salām,* peace be upon him.

ؓ following the name of a companion of the Prophet Muhammad, a saint, or *khalīfah* stands for *radiyallāhu 'anhu* or *'anhā,* may Allah be pleased with him or her.

(A) Indicates an Arabic word

(T) Indicates a Tamil word

ahādīth (A) (sing. *hadīth*) In Islam, authenticated accounts relating the deeds and utterances of the Prophet ﷺ. If the words or commands of Allah were received directly by the Prophet Muhammad ﷺ, it is known as a *hadīth qudsī.* Words of wisdom; discourse of wisdom. *Ahādīth* is sometimes used to refer to the traditional accounts of other prophets as well.

aham (T) The heart; the beauty of the heart.

aiyō (T) An exclamatory expression, "Oh no!"

ākhirah (A) The hereafter; the next world; the divine world; the kingdom of God.

'ālam (A) (pl. *'ālamīn*) World; cosmos; universe.

al-hamdu lillāh (A) All praise is to God. Allah is the glory and greatness that deserves all praise. "You are the One responsible for the appearance of all creations. Whatever appears, whatever disappears, whatever receives benefit or loss—all is Yours. I have surrendered everything into Your hands. I remain with hands outstretched, spread out, empty, and helpless. Whatever is happening and whatever is going to happen is all Yours."

alif (A) The first letter of the Arabic alphabet (ا). To the transformed man of wisdom, the *alif* represents Allah, the One.

'ālim(s) (A) Learned ones. *See also 'ulamā'.*

Allah or *Allāhu* (A) God; the One and Only; the One of infinite grace and incomparable love; the One who gives of His undiminishing wealth of grace; the One who is beyond comparison or example; the Eternal, Effulgent One; the One of overpowering effulgence.

Allāh-Muhammad (A) The station wherein Muhammad ﷺ becomes perfection, becomes complete. What is called Muhammad ﷺ is a "form" within which Allah resides and from within which He speaks. Muhammad ﷺ is absolutely united with Allah existing only as a vehicle for the manifestation of His essence and attributes.

Allāhu Akbar (A) God is great!

Allāhu ta'ālā Nāyan (A & T) God is the Lord above all. *Allāhu:* (A) Almighty God. *Ta'ālā:* (A) the One who exists in all lives in a state of humility and exaltedness. *Nāyan:* (T) the Ruler who protects and sustains.

ambiyā' (A) (sing. *nabī*) Prophets.

Āmīn (A) So be it. May He make this complete; may it be so.

anāthi (T) The beginningless beginning; the state in which God meditated upon Himself alone; the period before creation when Allah was alone in darkness, unaware of Himself even though everything was within Him; the state of unmanifestation, before the creation came forth.

anbu (T) Love.

'Arafāt (A) A plain which lies approximately ten miles southeast of Mecca. A major rite of *hajj* is the day of standing forth at *'Arafāt* on the 9th of *Dhul-Hijjah*. On this day the pilgrims pray to God and beg for forgiveness, in the same way that Adam and Eve ⟨﷿⟩ prayed to God on *Jabalur-Rahmah* (the Mount of Mercy), which is located at the eastern edge of the plain.

'arsh (A) The throne of God; the plenitude from which God rules; the station located on the crown of the head, which is the throne that can bear the weight of Allah. Allah is so heavy that we cannot carry the load with our hands or legs. The *'arsh* is the only part of the human being that can support Allah.

'arshul-mu'min (A) The throne of the true believer; the throne of one who has unshakable faith *(īmān)*; the throne of an *insān*, a human being who has that perfect certitude of *īmān*.

    Allah resides within the heart which praises Him and within the tongue which praises Him, the tongue which gives speech to only virtuous thoughts, the tongue which speaks the truth and praises the truth.

Ārumattavan (T) The One who has none to call His own. The One without the six *(āru)* evils.

arwāh (A) (sing. *rūh*) Souls; the light rays of God.

ash-hadu al-lā ilāha ill-Allāh wahdahu lā sharīka lah, wa ash-hadu anna Muhammadan 'abduhu wa rasūluh (A) I witness (testify) that there is no god except the One God and Muhammad is the Messenger of God. *See* Appendix: The Five *Kalimahs*.

'Āshūrā (A) The tenth day of *Muharram*, the day of the martyrdom of al-Husain ⟨﷿⟩, the son of 'Alī ⟨﷿⟩.

'asr (A) The afternoon prayer; the third of the five daily prayers in Islam.

as-salāmu 'alaikum wa rahmatullāhi wa barakātuhu kulluhu (A) May all the peace, the beneficence, and the blessings of God be upon you.

āthi (T) Primal beginning; the period after *anāthi;* the time when the *Qutb* (the wisdom which explains the truth of God) and the *Nūr* (the plenitude of the light of Allah) manifested within Allah; the time of the dawning of the light; the world of grace where the unmanifested begins to manifest in the form of resonance. In contrast to *awwal,* when the creations became manifest in form, *āthi* is the time when the first sound or vibration emerged.

a'ūdhu billāhi minash-shaitānir-rajīm (A) I seek refuge in God from the evils of the accursed satan. "Please annihilate satan from within me. Eliminate him from within me and burn him up. *Minal* (T) is the fire of the resplendent light that comes like lightning. In the same way that lightning strikes, burn him away from me. Burn satan who is the enemy to the children of Adam (ع). He is the one who has separated us from You, O God. Please prevent that enemy from coming and mingling within us. Prevent him from coming once again into our midst, and take us back to You."

auliyā' (A) (sing. *walī*) The favorites of God; those who are near to God; commonly used to refer to holy ones of Islam.

awwal (A) The time of the creation of forms; the stage at which the soul became surrounded by form and each creation took shape; the stage at which the souls of the six kinds of lives (earth life, fire life, water life, air life, ether life, and light life) were placed in their respective forms. Allah created these forms and then placed that entrusted treasure which is the soul within those forms.

āyat (A) (pl. *āyāt*) A verse in the *Qur'ān;* a sign or miracle.

Āyatul-Kursī (A) "The Verse of the Throne," Chapter II, Verse

255 of the Holy *Qur'ān*. Bawa Muhaiyaddeen has said that this is the only verse of the *Qur'ān* that satan cannot recite. Its power is so great that it would incinerate him.

Badushāh (Persian) Ruler; Emperor.

bahrul-'ilm (A) The ocean of divine knowledge.

Baitul-Muqaddas (A) A name given to the temple in Jerusalem on which site the Dome of the Rock stands today. Lit. the Holy House.

barakat (A) The wealth of Allah's grace.

Bismillāhir-Rahmānir-Rahīm (A) In the name of God, Most Merciful, Most Compassionate.
   Bismillāh: Allah, the first and the last; the One with a beginning and without a beginning. He is the One who is the cause for creation and for the absence of creation, the cause for the beginning and for the beginningless. He is the One who is completeness.
   Ar-Rahmān: He is the King, the Compassionate One, and the Beneficent One. He is the One who protects all creations and gives them nourishment. He looks after them, gives them love, takes them unto Himself, and comforts them. He gives them food, houses, property, and everything within Himself. He holds His creations within Himself and protects them. He is the One who reigns with justice.
   Ar-Rahīm: He is the One who redeems, the One who protects us from evil, the One who preserves and confers eternal bliss. No matter what we may do, He has the quality of forgiving us and accepting us back. He is the Tolerant One who forgives all the faults we have committed. He is the Savior. On the Day of Judgment, on the Day of Inquiry, and on all days since the beginning, He protects and brings His creations back unto Himself.

Bismin (A) A shortened form of *Bismillāhir-Rahmānir-Rahīm.*

buriyani (T) A traditional rice dish.

daulat (A) The wealth of the grace of Allah. The wealth of Allah is the wealth of divine knowledge *('ilm)* and the wealth of unshakable faith *(īmān)*.

dēva(s) (T) Celestial being.

dhāt (A) The essence of God; His treasury; His wealth of purity; His grace.

dhikr (A) The remembrance of God. It is a common name given to traditional prayers in praise of God. Of the many *dhikrs,* the most exalted *dhikr* is to say, *"Lā ilāha ill-Allāhu*—There is no god but God. Nothing exists other than God." All the others relate to His actions *(wilāyāt),* but this *dhikr* points to Him and to Him alone. *See also kalimah; Lā ilāha ill-Allāhu. See* Appendix: The Five *Kalimahs.*

du'ā' (A) A prayer of supplication.

dunyā (A) The earth-world in which we live; the world of physical existence; the darkness which separated from Allah at the time when the light of the *Nūr Muhammad* manifested from within Allah.

fard (A) (pl. *furūd)* Obligatory duty. *See also furūd.*

firdaus (A) The eighth heaven. If we can cut away the seven base desires known as the *nafs ammārah,* what remains will be Allah's qualities, actions, and conduct, His gracious attributes, and His duties. If man can make these his own and store them within his heart, then that is *firdaus.* That is Allah's house of infinite magnitude and perfect purity, a limitless heaven.

furūd (A) (sing. *fard)* Obligatory duties. The five *furūd* refer to the five pillars of Islam: *ash-shahādah* (witnessing that there is no god but God, and Muhammad is the Messenger of God), prayer, charity, fasting, and holy pilgrimage *(hajj).*

Allah has also given us six inner *furūd,* which the Sufis have explained. 1) If you go deep into Allah with the certitude of unwavering faith, you will see that within this eye of yours is an inner eye which can gaze upon Allah. 2) Within this nostril is a piece of flesh which can smell the fragrance of Allah. 3) Within this ear is a piece of flesh which can hear the sounds of Allah. 4) Within this tongue is a piece of flesh which can taste the beauty and the divine knowledge of Allah and know the taste of His wealth. 5) Within this tongue is also a voice which converses with Him and recites His remembrance in a state of total absorption. 6) And within this innermost heart is a piece of flesh where the eighteen thousand universes, the heavens, and His kingdom are found. It is there that the angels, the heavenly beings, prophets, and lights of Allah prostrate before Him.

gnānam (T) Divine wisdom. If a person can throw away all the worldly treasures and take within him only the treasure called Allah and His qualities and actions, His conduct and behavior, if he makes Allah the only treasure and completeness for him— that is the state of *gnānam.*

hadīth (A) *See ahādīth.*

hadrats (A) Honored ones; a term of great respect. The spiritual state of a prophet or a saint.

hajj (A) The holy pilgrimage to Mecca; the fifth *fard* (obligatory duty) in Islam. This duty must be done wearing the white shroud *(kafan)* of one who has died to the world. Before you undertake this pilgrimage, you must share your wealth among the poor. If you have a spouse and children, you must divide your wealth among them. True pilgrimage is to enter the state of dying before death. The inner desires must be surrendered and all of the self must die to make this pilgrimage.

Hajjiyar (A & T) A title used in Sri Lanka when someone has gone on the holy pilgrimage of *hajj.*

halāl (A) Permissible; those things that are permissible or lawful according to the commands of God and which conform to the word of God.

Hanal (T) The religion of fire worship.

harām (A) Forbidden; impermissible; that which is forbidden by truth, justice, and the commands of God. For those who are on the straight path, *harām* means all the evil things, actions, food, and dangers that can obstruct the path.

hasad (A) Jealousy.

hayāt (A) The plenitude of man's eternal life; the splendor of the completeness of life; the soul *(rūh)* of the splendor of man's life.

hayāt-maut (A) Life-death.

hayawān(s) (A) Beast.

Hijrah (A) The migration of Muhammad ⌖ from Mecca to Medina in 622 A. D., marking the beginning of the first Islamic state. The Prophet's custom of dating events from the *Hijrah* was later formalized and became the starting point of the Islamic, or *Hijrī,* calendar.

'ibādat (A) Worship and service to the One God.

ihrām (A) Pilgrim's shroud.

ill-Allāh (A) *See* Allah.

'ilm (A) Knowledge; divine knowledge; that secret knowledge, or light, that shines in the heart of the truly pious whereby one becomes enlightened.

imām (A) One who leads the congregation in the five-times prayer of Islam.

īmān (A) Absolute, complete, and unshakable faith, certitude, and determination that God alone exists; the complete acceptance by the heart that God is One.

Īmān-Islām (A) The state of the spotlessly pure heart which contains Allah's Holy *Qur'ān,* His divine radiance, His divine wisdom, His truth, His prophets, His angels, and His laws. The pure heart which, having cut away all evil, takes on the power of that courageous determination called faith and stands shining in the resplendence of Allah.

When the resplendence of Allah is seen as the completeness within the heart of man, that is *Īmān-Islām.* When the complete unshakable faith of the heart is directed toward the One who is completeness; when that completeness is made to merge with the One who is completeness; when that heart communes with that One, trusts only in Him, and worships only Him, accepting only Him and nothing else as the only perfection and the only One worthy of worship—that is *Īmān-Islām.*

insān(s) (A) Man; a human being. The true form of man is the form of Allah's qualities, actions, conduct, behavior, and virtues. The one who has realized the completeness of this form, having filled himself with these qualities, is truly an *insān.*

Insān-Qur'ān (A) The inner form of the human being is the *Qur'ān,* and it is linked together by the twenty-eight letters. This is the *Ummul-Qur'ān,* the source of the *Qur'ān.* It is the *Qur'ān* in which the revelations are revealed. The sounds in the *Qur'ān* which resonate through wisdom, the Messenger of Allah, Prophet Muhammad ﷺ, the angels, and the heavenly beings— all are made to exist in this body as secrets.

'ishā' (A) The night prayer, which is the fifth of the five daily prayers of Islam.

Islam (A) Spotless purity; the state of absolute purity; to accept the commands of God, His qualities, and His actions, and to establish that state within oneself. To cut away desire, to accept Him and know Him without the slightest doubt, and then to worship Him alone is Islam. To strengthen one's *īmān;* to accept *Lā ilāha ill-Allāhu* (There is no god but God) with absolute certitude, and to affirm this *kalimah*—that is the state of Islam. Also, the religion or creed of Islam.

Ka'bah (A) The *Ka'bah,* also known as the House of God *(Baitullāh),* is the central point toward which all Muslims turn to pray five times a day and is also the object of pilgrimage *(hajj),* the fifth *fard* (obligatory duty) of Islam. This cube-like building was originally built by Adam ﷺ in what is now the city of Mecca and has been rebuilt numerous times throughout the ages, most notably by Prophet Abraham ﷺ and his son, the Prophet Ishmael ﷺ. The Prophet Muhammad ﷺ was commanded by God to cleanse the Holy House of all idols and to restore its original purity and sanctity.

Within the human being, the *Kab'ah* represents the heart *(qalb),* the original source of prayer. It is the place in which a true human being meets God face to face. Like the outer *Ka'bah,* this sanctuary, too, must be cleansed of idols and restored to its original purity as the house in which God abides.

kafan (A) A cloth shroud that is wound around a corpse.

kāfir (A) One who conceals Allah's truth; one who fails to live according to Allah's qualities and virtues although being aware of what Allah has commanded and forbidden; one who is ungrateful or who rejects Allah after having awareness of the truth; one who worships things as equal to Allah, falling under the power of his base desires. Such a one hides the truth out of purely selfish motives, turning the heart into the form of darkness, falling prey to the forces of satan, and acquiring the qualities of satan.

kalām (A) Word; God's word.

kalimah (A) The affirmation of faith—*Lā ilāha ill-Allāhu:* There is no god but God. Other than God nothing exists.

The recitation or remembrance of God which cuts away the influence of the five elements (earth, fire, water, air, and ether),

washes away all the *karma* that has accumulated from the very
beginning until now, dispels the darkness, beautifies the heart,
and makes it resplend. The *kalimah* washes the body and the
heart of man and makes him pure, makes his wisdom emerge,
and impels that wisdom to know the self and God. *See also
dhikr; Lā ilāha ill-Allāhu. See also* Appendix: The Five *Kalimahs.*

Karbalā' (A) When Allah ordered the Angel 'Izrā'īl ⓐ to take a
handful of earth, from which Adam ⓐ was created, that handful of earth gathered from all four directions was placed in
Karbalā', the center of the eighteen thousand universes.

It is also a city located in Iraq, which throughout the ages has
been a battlefield. It is where al-Husain ⓐ, the son of 'Alī ⓐ,
fought against his enemies and was killed. On a symbolic level,
Karbalā' signifies the battlefield of the heart *(qalb).*

karma (T) The inherited qualities formed at the time of conception; the qualities of the essence of the five elements; the qualities of the mind; the qualities of the connection to hell; the
qualities and actions of the seventeen *purānas* which are: arrogance, *karma,* and *māyā,* or illusion; the three sons of *māyā*
(tārahan, singhan, and *sūran),* the six intrinsic evils of desire, anger, greed, attachment, bigotry, and envy, and the five acquired
evils of intoxication, lust, theft, murder, and falsehood.

khair (A) That which is right or good; that which is acceptable to
wisdom and to Allah, as opposed to *sharr,* that which is evil or
bad.

kursī (A) The gnostic eye; the eye of light; the center of the forehead where Allah's resplendence *(Nūr)* was impressed on
Adam's ⓐ forehead. Lit. the "footstool" or seat of the resplendence of Allah.

Lā ilāha ill-Allāh, Muhammadur-Rasūlullāh (A) There is no god
but God, and Muhammad is the Messenger of God. *See also*
Appendix: The Five *Kalimahs.*

Lā ilāha ill-Allāhu (A) There is no god but God. Other than God nothing exists. To accept this with certitude, to strengthen one's unshakable faith *(īmān),* and to affirm this *kalimah* is the state of Islam.

There are two aspects. *Lā ilāha* is the manifestation of creation *(sifāt). Ill-Allāhu* is the essence *(dhāt).* All that has appeared, all creation, belongs to *lā ilāha.* The name of the One who created all that is *ill-Allāhu.* Lit. No god (is), except the One God. *See also dhikr; kalimah. See also* Appendix: The Five *Kalimahs.*

labbaik (A) "Here I am." The opening words of the *Talbiyah,* the most frequently used prayer for the pilgrimage *(hajj)* and the lesser pilgrimage *('umrah).* When Abraham ⊕ was directed by Allah to rebuild the *Ka'bah,* he was also told to call the people to the house of Allah to worship Him alone. The *Talbiyah* is an answer, an acknowledgment to this call. *See also* Appendix: *Labbaik.*

lām (A) The Arabic letter (ل) which corresponds to the English consonant 'l'. In the transformed man of wisdom, *lām* represents the *Nūr,* the resplendence of Allah.

lebbe (A) One who does service in a mosque and performs various duties within that mosque.

maghrib (A) The fourth of the five daily prayers in Islam, which begins just after sunset.

mahr (A) Dowry.

malā'ikat (A) (sing. *malak*) Bawa Muhaiyaddeen ⊕ frequently uses this word to mean the chosen, selected, or advanced heavenly beings, referred to as archangels. Lit. angels.

malak (A) (pl. *malā'ikat*) Angel.

mantra(s) (T) An incantation or formula; the recitation of a magic word or set of words; sounds imbued with force or energy, through constant repetition, but limited to the energy of the five elements. (The *kalimah* is not a *mantra.*)

maut (A) Death.

māyā (T) Illusion; the unreality of the visible world; the glitters seen in the darkness of illusion; the 105 million glitters seen in the darkness of the mind which result in 105 million rebirths. *Māyā* is an energy, or *shakti,* which takes on various shapes, causes man to forfeit his wisdom, and confuses and hypnotizes him into a state of torpor. It can take many, many millions of hypnotic forms. If man tries to grasp one of these forms with his intellect, although he sees the form he will never catch it, for it will elude him by taking on yet another form.

mihrāb (A) The prayer niche in front of a mosque indicating the direction of Mecca. The third verb form derived from the same root means to wage war. Thus, the *mihrāb* is the point of focus which is the instrument in waging the inner war against that which is other than Allah.

Mīkā'īl ⊜ (A) Michael, the archangel of water.

mīm (A) The Arabic letter (ρ) which corresponds to the English consonant 'm'. In the transformed man of wisdom, *mīm* represents Muhammad ⊜. The shape of *mīm* is like a sperm cell and from this comes the *nuqtah,* or dot, which is the form of the world.

Mi'rāj (A) The mystical journey of the Prophet Muhammad ⊜ through the heavens which took place in the twelfth year of the Prophet's ⊜ mission on the twenty-seventh day of the month of *Rajab.* During this event the divine order for five-times prayer was given. Lit. an ascent.

Mount 'Arafāt (A) *See* 'Arafāt.

mu'adhdhin(s) (A) The one who makes the call to prayer for the five daily prayers of Islam.

mubārakāt (A) The supreme, imperishable treasure of all three worlds *(awwal, dunyā,* and *ākhirah).* Lit. blessings.

Muhaiyaddeen 🕮 or *Muhyiddīn* (A) The pure resplendence called the *Qutb* 🕮. The one who manifests the wisdom which lies hidden and buried under illusion. The one who revives the life of wisdom and gives it to others. *See also Qutb.*

muham (T) Face; the beauty of the face.

Muhammadur-Rasūlullāh 🕮 (A) Prophet Muhammad 🕮, the Messenger of God.

Muharram (A) The first month of the Muslim calendar.

mu'min(s) (A) A true believer; one of pure faith.

Mustafā (A) The chosen one; the selected one.

Mustafar-Rasūl 🕮 (A) The Chosen Messenger, Prophet Muhammad 🕮.

nafs or *nafs ammārah* (A) The seven kinds of base desires. That is, desires meant to satisfy one's own pleasure and comfort. All thoughts are contained within the *ammārah*. *Ammārah* is like the mother while the *nafs* are like children. Lit. person; spirit; inclination or desire which goads or incites toward evil.

Nūr (A) Light; the resplendence of Allah; the plenitude of the light of Allah which has the brilliance of a hundred million suns; the completeness of Allah's qualities. When the plenitude of all these becomes one and resplends as one, that is the *Nūr,* that is Allah's qualities and His beauty. It is the resplendent wisdom which is innate in man and can be awakened.

Nūr Muhammad (A) The beauty of the qualities and actions of the powers *(wilāyāt)* of Allah, the radiance of Allah's essence *(dhāt)* which shines within the resplendence of His truth. It was the light of Muhammad 🕮 called *Nūr Muhammad* that was impressed upon the forehead of Adam 🕮. Of the nine aspects of Muhammad 🕮, *Nūr Muhammad* is that aspect which is the wisdom.

olis (T) Lights of God.

pūjā(s) (T) Ritual prayer or worship.

qalb (A) Heart; the heart within the heart of man; the innermost heart. Bawa Muhaiyaddeen ☽ explains that there are two states for the *qalb*. In one state the *qalb* is made up of four chambers which are earth, fire, air, and water—representing Hinduism, Fire Worship, Christianity, and Islam. Inside these four chambers is the second state, the flower of the *qalb* which is the divine qualities of God. This is the flower of grace *(rahmat)*. God's fragrance exists within this inner *qalb*.

qiblah (A) The direction one faces in prayer; internally, it is the throne of God within the heart *(qalb)*.

Qiyāmah (A) The standing forth; Day of Reckoning; Day of Questioning.

qudrat (A) Power; the power of God's grace and the qualities which control all other forces.

Qur'ān (A) The words of God that were revealed to His Messenger, Prophet Muhammad ☽; those words that came from His power are called the *Qur'ān;* God's inner book of the heart; the light and lives of God's grace which came as the resonance from Allah; that which resonated from Him and became understood; that which never dies; that light and power which are His one hundred glorious names and His form *(sūrat)*. He gives it life, and that is the *Nūr,* or the wisdom which explains. That is the Guru which is the light, and the *Rasūl* ☽. It is the beautiful light which has to be understood from inside.

Qutb(s) (A) Divine analytic wisdom; the wisdom which explains; that which measures the length and breadth of the seven oceans of the *nafs,* or base desires; that which awakens all the truths which have been destroyed and buried in the ocean of illusion *(māyā);* that which awakens true faith, certitude, and determination *(īmān);* that which gives explanations to life *(hayāt);* the state of purity as it existed in the beginning of creation *(awwal);* the grace of the essence of God *(dhāt),* which awakens the life *(hayāt)* of purity and transforms it into the divine vibration.

Qutb is also a name which has been given to Allah. He can be addressed as *Yā Qutb* or *Yā Quddūs,* the Holy One. *Quddūs* is His power or miracle *(wilāyat),* while *Qutb* is His action. *Wilāyat* is the power of that action. Lit. axis; axle; pole; pivot; a title used for the great holy men of Islam.

qutbiyyat (A) The wisdom of the *Qutb;* the sixth level of conscious-ness; divine analytic wisdom; the wisdom which explains the truth of God.

Rabb (A) God; the Lord; the Creator and Protector.

Rabbil-'ālamīn (A) Lord of all the universes.

ar-Rahīm (A) The Most Compassionate; the Sustainer and Re-deemer; one of the ninety-nine beautiful names of God. He is the One who is full of endless compassion for all lives. *See also Bismillāhir-Rahmānir-Rahīm.*

ar-Rahmān (A) The Merciful One.

rahmat (A) God's grace; His mercy; His forgiveness and compas-sion; His benevolence; His wealth. To all creations, He is the wealth of life *(hayāt)* and the wealth of unshakable faith *(īmān).* All the good things that we receive from God are His *rahmat.* That is the wealth of God's plenitude. Everything that is within God is *rahmat,* and if He were to give that grace, that would be an undiminishing, limitless wealth.

Rahmatul-'ālamīn (A) The Mercy and Compassion of all the uni-verses; the One who gives everything to all His creations.

Ramadān (A) The month of fasting which is the fourth *fard* (obligatory duty) of Islam.

Rasūl ⌣ (A) The Messenger of Allah, Prophet Muhammad ⌣; God's essence *(dhāt),* the resplendence that emerged from

His effulgence, shining radiantly as His Messenger ⊕. Muhammad ⊕, the manifestation of that resplendence, discourses on the explanations of luminous wisdom which he imparts to Allah's creations. He is the one who begs for truth from Allah and intercedes with prayers for all of Allah's creations and for his followers. Therefore, Allah has anointed His *Rasūl,* the Prophet Muhammad ⊕, with the title: *The Messenger who is the savior for both worlds.*

The word *rasūl* can be used to refer to any of Allah's apostles or messengers.

Rasūlullāh ⊕ (A) The Messenger of Allah; a title used for Prophet Muhammad ⊕.

rishi(s) (T) Ascetic; sage; poet. Bawa Muhaiyaddeen ⊕ explains that *rishis, muktars,* and *siddhars* are all the same—they perform miracles and magics.

rūh (A) The soul; the light ray of God; the light of God's wisdom. Bawa Muhaiyaddeen ⊕ explains that *rūh* is life *(hayāt).* Out of the six kinds of lives it is the light life, the ray of the light of the resplendence of Allah, the *Nūr,* which does not die or disappear. It is the truth. The other five lives appear and disappear. That which exists forever without death is the soul. It is Allah's grace *(rahmat)* which has obtained the wealth of the imperishable treasure of all three worlds *(mubārakāt).*

rūhānī (A) Elemental spirit arising from desires; the spirit of the elements. There are six kinds of lives within man. One is the human life which is the light-life. That is the soul *(rūh).* Associated with this are the lives of earth, fire, water, air, and ether. These constitute the *rūhānī.*

rukū' (A) A posture in the daily formal *salāt* (prayer) of Islam, where one bends over from the torso, with head down and hands resting on knees.

rupee(s) (T) Unit of money in Sri Lanka and India.

sabab (A) Meaning; reason.

sabūr (A) Inner patience; to go within patience, to accept it, to think and reflect within it. *Sabūr* is that patience deep within patience which comforts, soothes, and alleviates mental suffering.

Yā *Sabūr*—one of the ninety-nine names of Allah. God, who in a state of limitless patience, is always forgiving the faults of His created beings and continuing to protect them.

sadaqah (A) Charity; contributions to the poor; the third *fard* (obligatory duty) of Islam, which requires Muslims to give a certain percentage of their income to the needy and poor. True charity is to recognize the lives of others to be as valuable as one's own and to comfort and care for them as one would for oneself.

sajdah (A) Prostration in prayer.

salām(s) (A) Peace; the peace of God. Greetings! When one gives *salāms* to another, it means in God's name or in the presence of God, may both of us become one without any division; both of us are in a state of unity, a state of peace.

salāt (A) Blessing or prayer. Specifically, the prayer that is done five times daily by Muslims.

salawāt (A) (sing. *salāt*) Prayers; blessings; glorification. The practice of praying to, praising, and glorifying Allah, and invoking peace and blessings upon the *Rasūl* (ﷺ), the prophets, and the angels.

The praise that you offer to Allah, the *Rasūl* (ﷺ), and the heavenly beings comes back to you as your own treasure, your own wealth. The *salāms* and *salawāt* you offer come back to you and light up your own face and heart. This is the reason that the *salawāt* is considered to be something very exalted.

sallallāhu 'alaihi wa sallam (A) God bless him and grant him peace. A supplication traditionally spoken after mentioning the name of Prophet Muhammad. In text usually denoted with Arabic calligraphy.

sannyāsis (T) Renunciates; ascetics.

sayyid(s) (A) A descendant of Prophet Muhammad ﷺ.

shaikh (A) A spiritual guide or master; one, who knowing himself and God, guides others on the straight path, the path to God.

shaitān (A) Satan.

shaitāniyyat (A) The state of being *shaitān.*

shakti(s) (T) Elemental energy; force.

shakūr (A) Gratitude; contentment; contentment arising from gratitude; the state within the inner patience known as *sabūr;* that which is stored within the treasure chest of patience.
   Yā Shakūr—one of the ninety-nine beautiful names of Allah. To have *shakūr* with the help of the One who is *Yā Shakūr* is true *shakūr.*

sharr (A) That which is wrong, bad, or evil, as opposed to *khair,* that which is good.

siddhis (T) Magics; miracles; supernatural abilities or feats. The capacity to perform miracles obtained by devotion to and control of the elements.

sifāt (A) (sing. *sifat*) That which arose from the word "Be!" *(Kun!);* all that has come into being as form. Depending on the context, the word *sifāt* may mean the creations, the manifestations of God, or the attributes of God.

subh (A) The first of the five daily prayers in Islam. Also known as *fajr.*

Sūfiyyat (A) The fifth level of spiritual ascendence. The state of one who has transcended the four religions and has merged with God.

In the station of *Sūfiyyat,* one speaks without talking, sees without looking, hears without listening, relishes fragrances without smelling, and learns without studying. That knowing cannot be learned, and that understanding cannot be acquired by mere study. These and many other such states come with acquiring the qualities of God and losing oneself within those qualities. Although one still exists within the body, he has built within himself the palace of divine luminous wisdom. One who has perfected this state is a Sufi.

suhūr (A) A reference to the last meal which is taken during *Ramadān,* beginning the day's fast.

sukūn (A) A graphic symbol, resembling a tiny circle (°) which denotes a consonant with no vowel. Lit. silent; quiet.

sunīyam (T) Black magic; sorcery; enchantment; ceremonial defilement; illusory vacuum; chasm.

sunnah (A) The sayings and practices of the *Rasūl* ⫩ or other prophets.

sūrat (A) Form or shape, such as the form of man (spelled with the Arabic letter *sād).*

sūrat (A) A chapter of the *Qur'ān* (spelled with the Arabic letter *sīn).* Lit. row; series.

sūratud-dunyā (A) The form of the world.

Sūratul-Baqarah (A) The second *sūrat* of the *Qur'ān,* which contains the *Āyatul-Kursī.*

Sūratul-Fātihah (A) The opening chapter of the *Qur'ān;* the inner form of man; the clarity of understanding the four elements of the body (earth, fire, water, and air), and the realization of the self and of Allah within. The *Sūratul-Fātihah* is recited at the beginning of every prayer. Within man is the *Sūratul-Fātihah,* and within the *Sūratul-Fātihah* is the inner form of man. If we split open that form, we can see within it Allah's words, His qualities, His actions, His three thousand divine attributes, and His ninety-nine powers *(wilāyāt)*. That is the inner form of man *(sūratul-insān)*.

The *Sūratul-Fātihah* must be split open with wisdom to see all these within. It must be opened by the ocean of divine knowledge *(bahrul-'ilm)*. Opening his heart *(qalb)*, opening his form *(sūrat)* and looking within, having his own form looking at his own form—that is the *Sūratul-Fātihah*. What is recited on the outside is the *Al-hamdu Sūrat*. The outer meaning is on the first level of spiritual ascendance *(sharī'at);* the inner meaning relates to the essence *(dhāt)*. *Fātihah* means literally to open out. It is opening the heart and looking within.

Sūratur-Rahmān (A) A chapter of the *Qur'ān*.

Sūrat Yā Sīn (A) A chapter of the *Qur'ān* often referred to as the heart of the *Qur'ān*.

swamiars (T) Holy men.

swarnam and *swarkam* (T) Heaven (different levels).

tantra(s) (T) A trick; a cunning trick performed with a selfish motive of self-praise or self-gain.

tārahan, singhan, and *sūran* (T) The three sons of illusion *(māyā)*. *Tārahan* is the trench or the pathway for the sexual act, the birth canal or vagina. *Singhan* is the arrogance present at the moment when the semen is ejaculated. It is the quality of the lion. *Sūran* is the illusory images of the mind enjoyed at the moment of ejaculation. It is all the qualities and energies of the mind.

tasbīh (A) Glorification of God; offering prayers of praise.

taubah (A) Repentance; to ask God's pardon for sins and errors, to turn away from them, and to vow not to commit them again.

tawāf(s) (A) The ritual circumambulation which is done seven times around the *Ka'bah* in Mecca.

tawakkul or *tawakkul-'alallāh* (A) Absolute trust in God; surrender to God; handing over to God the entire responsibility for everything. *Al-Wakīl* is one of the ninety-nine beautiful names of Allah: the Trustee, the Guardian.

thambi(s) (T) Little or younger brother.

thollay (T) Trouble or difficulty.

Tiru Qur'ān (A) Also called *Tiru Marai* (T) The Original *Qur'ān;* the Inner *Qur'ān* inscribed within the heart. All the secrets *(sirr)* and the essence *(dhāt)* from the three worlds (the beginning of creation, or *awwal,* this physical world, or *dunyā,* and the hereafter, or *ākhirah)* have been buried and concealed within the *Qur'ān* by Allah. There, He has concealed the explanations of the essence of grace *(dhāt)* and of the manifestations of creation *(sifāt).* There He has concealed the *alif, lām, mīm;* these three are the *dhāt.* That is why it is called the *Tiru Qur'ān. (Tiru* means triple in Tamil.) All of everything is contained within that *Qur'ān.* All of Allah's wealth is contained there, and all His *wilāyāt* (powers) are present in their fullness in the *Qur'ān,* the *Tiru Qur'ān.*

toluhai (T) The performance of prayer where one remembers only God to the exclusion of everything else. Also refers to the five-times prayer of Islam.

ulaham (T) World.

ul-aham (T) Inner heart.

'ulamā' (A) (sing. *'ālim)* Teachers; learned ones; scholars.

ummī (A) Silent; unlettered.

Ummul-Qur'ān (A) The 'source' or 'mother' of the *Qur'ān.* It is used commonly to refer to the *Sūratul-Fātihah,* or the opening chapter of the *Qur'ān.* It is said that within the 124 letters of the *Sūratul-Fātihah* is contained the meaning of the entire *Qur'ān.* It is often used to denote the eternal source of all the revelations to all of the prophets and is also known as the *Ummul-Kitāb* (the mother, or source, of the book). This is a divine, indestructible tablet on which all is recorded. This is the silent *Qur'ān* which exists as a mystery within the heart *(qalb)* of each person.

wahy (A) Revelation; inspiration from God; the inspired word of God revealed to a prophet; the commandments or words of God transmitted by the Archangel Gabriel ﷺ. *Wahys,* or revelations, have come to Adam ﷺ, Moses ﷺ, and various other prophets, but especially to Prophet Muhammad ﷺ. Muhammad ﷺ received 6,666 revelations. The histories of each of the earlier prophets were contained within the revelations given to Prophet Muhammad ﷺ.

waqt(s) (A) Time of prayer. In the religion of Islam there are five specified *waqts,* or times of prayer, each day. But truly, there is only one *waqt.* That is the prayer that never ends, wherein one is in direct communication with God and one is merged with God.

wāw (A) The Arabic letter (و) corresponding to the English consonant 'w'. In the human form made of the twenty-eight Arabic letters, the *'wāw'* denotes the genital area.

wilāyat (A) (pl. *wilāyāt*) God's power; that which has been revealed and manifested through God's actions; the miraculous names and actions of God; the powers of His attributes through which all creations came into existence.

Yā (A) The vocative 'O'. An exclamation of praise; a title of greatness or praise.

Yā Rabbal-'ālamīn (A) O Ruler of the universes! The Creator who nourishes and protects all of His creations forever.

zamzam (A) The spring which God caused to flow in order to provide water for Hagar ﷺ, and Ishmael ﷺ, when they were alone in the desert. Later Abraham ﷺ and Ishmael ﷺ built the *Ka'bah* next to this spring which is still there today. It is said to flow from the spring of abundance *(al-Kauthar)* in paradise.

zuhr (A) The second of the five daily prayers of Islam, which is performed after the sun begins to decline in midday.

Index

Books by
M. R. Bawa Muhaiyaddeen ﴿رَضِيَ﴾

To Die Before Death: The Sufi Way of Life

A Song of Muhammad ﷺ

Gems of Wisdom series—
Vol. 1: The Value of Good Qualities
Vol. 2: Beyond Mind and Desire
Vol. 3: The Innermost Heart
Vol. 4: Come to Prayer

A Contemporary Sufi Speaks—
To Teenagers and Parents
On the Signs of Destruction
On Peace of Mind
On the True Meaning of Sufism
On Unity: The Legacy of the Prophets
The Meaning of Fellowship
Mind, Desire, and the Billboards of the World

Foreign Language Publications—
Ein Zeitgenössischer Sufi Spricht über Inneren Frieden
(A Contemporary Sufi Speaks on Peace of Mind—
German Translation)

Deux Discours tirés du Livre L'Islam et la Paix Mondiale:
Explications d'un Soufi
(Two Discourses from the Book Islam and World Peace:
Explanations of a Sufi—French Translation)

For free catalog or book information call:
(888) 786-1786

About the
Bawa Muhaiyaddeen Fellowship

Muhammad Raheem Bawa Muhaiyaddeen ☺ a Sufi mystic from Sri Lanka, was a man of extraordinary wisdom and compassion. For over seventy years he shared his knowledge and experience with people of every race and religion and from all walks of life.

The central branch of The Bawa Muhaiyaddeen Fellowship is located in Philadelphia, Pennsylvania. It was Bawa Muhaiyaddeen's residence while he was in the United States until his death in December 1986. The Fellowship continues to serve as a meeting house and a reservoir of people and materials for all who are interested in his teachings.

Also located on the same property is The Mosque of Shaikh Muhammad Raheem Bawa Muhaiyaddeen where the daily five times of prayer and Friday congregational prayers are held. An hour west of the Fellowship is the *Mazār*, or tomb, of M. R. Bawa Muhaiyaddeen which is open for visitation.

For further information write or phone:

The Bawa Muhaiyaddeen Fellowship
5820 Overbrook Avenue
Philadelphia, Pennsylvania 19131

(215) 879-8604
(24 hour answering machine)

E-mail Address: info@bmf.org
Web Address: http://www.bmf.org

If you would like to visit the Fellowship or obtain a schedule of current events or branch locations and meetings, please write, phone, or E-mail *Attn: Visitor Information.*